The Trip to
Bethlehem

The Traditional Christmas Story as a Guide to Spiritual Transformation

The Trip to
Bethlehem

The Traditional Christmas Story as a Guide to Spiritual Transformation

Hypatia Hasbrouck

unity®
Books

Unity Village, MO 64065-0001

The Trip to Bethlehem
Second Edition, 2021

Unity Books are available at special discounts for bulk purchases for study groups, book clubs, sales promotions, book signings, or fundraising. To place an order, call the Unity Customer Care Department at 816-251-3571 or email *wholesaleaccts@unityonline.org*.

Cover design: Laura Carl

Interior Design: Perfection Press

Library of Congress No. 2021938269

ISBN 978-0-87159-415-0

Canada GST R132529033

In loving memory of

My grandmother, Emma Dunton,

and my mother, Millicent Dunton Hogg,

who "bent the twig" in the direction of New Thought,

and for

All my fellow travelers, known and unknown,

on the mystical trip to Bethlehem.

Table of Contents

Acknowledgments

Many people made the writing and publication of this book possible. I am grateful to Rev. Edward "Ed" Rabel, who opened my understanding to the significant meanings hidden in the stories in both the Hebrew and Christian scriptures. In his classes on the metaphysical interpretation of the Bible and *The Twelve Powers of Man* at the Unity ministerial school, I gained the mental tools for metaphysical interpretation.

I am grateful to Rev. Philip White and Rev. Michael Maday, who encouraged me to publish my work on the Christmas story; to Rev. Sallye Taylor, who introduced me to the work of Fritz Kunkel; to Rev. Martha Giudici, who introduced me to various forms of meditation; to Rev. Nan Wire, my sister, who introduced me to the concept of coping roles; to Dr. Janet Davis, psychologist, who clarified Jungian symbolism for me; to my friend, Marge King, who graciously put her computer and the computerized Bible concordance at my disposal; and to my friend Marilyn Morris, who supports me morally and materially in every undertaking.

—Hypatia Hasbrouck

Foreword

The Christmas story is one of the great phenomena of our lives. In actual practice or in mind, we follow the route of wise men and kneel with shepherds to celebrate that night of stars and angels when a child was born in Bethlehem. Yet even for the most literal-minded person, something much deeper is stirring and our souls seem to know it. In this wonderful book, Hypatia Hasbrouck has blended the traditions of the past with the rich journey of her own work in understanding so that we might be able to internalize this glorious pageant.

When we lay all the error of life onto other people, we never see what we do to participate in our own lives. Until we recognize what is going on inside ourselves, we constantly blame everyone else for our problems and do not realize that we, too, can be part of the problem. Similarly, we can project all our divinity onto church people or holy places or people of the past, and not realize that the power of the Divine can be felt and known inside ourselves.

This powerful book invites you to experience the drama of Christmas in the most profound way inside yourself, so that you find all the characters and all the pieces of the story are parts of who you are.

In this bigger story, Christmas lives in you, and indeed your soul is born in a new way. After you read this book, Christmas will never be the same for you, and your whole life will be richer.

Welcome to an amazing trip to Bethlehem.

—Rev. V. Stanford Hampson

Introduction

The seed idea for *The Trip to Bethlehem* was planted during a trip to the Holy Land before I began studying for the Unity ministry.

It was in the spring of 1966, one year before the Six-Day War. At the time, I was teaching in the Teheran American School in Iran, an Islamic nation, so I could not travel to Israel from there but had to fly to Jordan. It did not matter to me. Jerusalem was a divided city, and the Old City—the part where all the historical places are located—was in Jordan, as were most of the other places I wished to visit.

Because Bethlehem then was in Jordanian territory, my route to Bethlehem was longer than the one the Magi made from Jerusalem to Bethlehem. They traveled only six miles on a route that rose and fell only a few feet along the way, but the road that follows their ancient route lay in Israeli territory. So the tour car in which I traveled had to go 18 miles, winding down into the Kidron Valley and then back up to the plateau on which both Jerusalem and Bethlehem are situated.

Even then I could see symbolism in the fact that the conflict between Jordan and Israel had tripled the length of the journey between the city whose name means "habitation of peace" and the birthplace of the Prince of Peace.

Not long after my visit to the Holy Land, a series of outer events triggered an inner process in me that led to my entering the ministerial school at Unity Village, Missouri, six years later. In the years since then, I have come to understand the many metaphysical implications in the facts of my first ride from Jerusalem to Bethlehem.

It was metaphysically significant that the whole first round trip to Bethlehem took place in Jordan. According to the *Metaphysical Bible Dictionary*, the name *Jordan* means "the descender; the south flowing; flowing (river) of judgment." In his discussion of the metaphysical meaning of Jordan, Unity cofounder Charles Fillmore says that it refers to the "stream of thought constantly flowing through the subconscious *(the south flowing)*, made up of thoughts good, bad, and indifferent, which is typified in Scripture by the river Jordan ... This thought stream has to be crossed before the children of Israel can go over into the Promised Land, before the true, real thoughts of the organism can enter into the divine substance and life in the subconsciousness." The name *Israel*, according to the *Metaphysical Bible Dictionary*, means "striving for God; dominion with God." In his discussion of the metaphysical meaning of Israelites, Fillmore says they are "the illumined thoughts in consciousness, which are undergoing spiritual discipline."

In 1966, within me there was a considerable conflict between the states of consciousness symbolized by Jordan and Israel. I suspect that I am not much different from most people, and that we will always have some conflict between the inner Jordan and Israel.

Just as the historical conflict had forced tourists to take the longer route from Jerusalem to the traditional birthplace of Jesus, so do our thoughts and feelings lengthen and complicate our mystical trip to the true birthplace of the Christ, if we are still, metaphysically speaking, in Jordan and even if we start from a place of inner peace.

I made my second trip to Bethlehem in the summer of 1982 as one of the tour leaders for a group of Unity people on a trip to Egypt and Israel. There was still conflict between Jordan and Israel, but Jerusalem was no longer divided, and Bethlehem and other places we wished to visit were now in Israeli territory. Friends and families were nervous to see us set off for an area of the world in a state of unrest. However, on the day we flew from Cairo to Tel Aviv, a 10-day cease-fire was declared. It lasted until about one-half hour after we left Tel Aviv for New York.

The tour group chose to take the long route from Jerusalem to Bethlehem, because there are points of historical interest in the Kidron Valley, but we could and did take the wise men's route back from Bethlehem to Jerusalem.

Once again, to me the outer events had metaphysical significance. For one reason or another, we do seem to prefer to take a more complicated journey than is necessary to reach our inner Bethlehem, but once we have arrived, the journey to the habitation of peace is easy and short.

Also, in 1982, there was a cease-fire between my inner Jordan and Israel. The metaphysical cease-fire has been declared within me many times through the ensuing years, and when I experience it, inner peace is easy to reach.

It is my belief that as, one by one, people take their mystical trips to Bethlehem, together we can achieve the inner peace that produces the kind of consciousness that supports peace-making efforts in the outer world.

The Christmas
Myth

1

This Is Our Story

The Christmas story is our story, not the one in the Gospel According to Matthew nor the one in the Gospel According to Luke, but the traditional Christmas story. The traditional Christmas story combines those two contradictory accounts with details added during the first few centuries of the Christian era into a design for the spiritual growth of anyone. That is the story that can be ours—yours, mine, and everyone else's, whether or not the person is Christian.

Each year, the traditional Christmas story stirs believers and unbelievers alike, not only because it celebrates the birth of the Christ child—the baby who grew into the man whose life and teachings changed the course of history and shaped the mind and culture of the Western world—but also because it appeals to the very depths of our being. It stirs all of us because the Christ child represents the higher Self, the true Self, of everyone. That child is within us and, in our depths, we know that at some time we are destined to take the mystical trip to our inner Bethlehem, the birthplace of our own higher Self.

All biblical stories, historical or not, have three levels of meaning. The first level is the obvious, literal meaning—in journalistic terms, the who, what, when, where, and perhaps how or why or both. The second level is the moral meaning—the implied lesson about the consequences of our choices and behavior when dealing with other persons or natural forces, when pursuing our own goals, or when complying with or attempting to defy God's activity. The third level is the metaphysical meaning—the implied lesson about the psychological and spiritual growth and development of any human being. At this level, everything in the story symbolizes something that can or does exist or can happen or does happen within the total consciousness of any person.

On the literal level, the Christmas story recounts a series of miraculous events that culminate in the appearance of the only person to be, paradoxically, "fully human and fully divine" in the words of many Christian leaders. On the moral level, it shows what happens when people cooperate with God's plan, as did Elizabeth, Mary, and Joseph. (Because the purpose of this book is to show readers how to use the story as a guide to spiritual transformation, the moral level will receive no further attention.) On the metaphysical level, the story is an invitation to a mystical journey to the place within ourselves where we can find our full humanity and our own divinity—the inner Christ, our higher Self.

The higher Self is called the Christ because the word *Christ* comes from a Greek word for "anointed" or "chosen." The Hebrew equivalent is *messiah*. Either word denotes the image of God, the spiritual idea or pattern for the Self of every human being. In that sense, each of us is chosen to express the image of God. The image of God within us imbues us with life and intelligence and eternally connects us to the source of all power and substance.

As the pattern we are designed to fulfill, the higher Self is the matrix for the smaller self that we call the *ego*. The ego forms in response to the use of a godlike attribute we exercise to some extent every day—free will. God is absolutely free, and, because we have the image of God within us, we have freedom of choice. Like God, we have infinite possibilities within us. We may freely choose which possibilities to express and how to express them. When we choose wisely, we are gradually led to the place in consciousness where the Christ becomes alive in us.

That is the deeper meaning of the story that has evolved from and expands upon the New Testament accounts of the birth of Jesus. The story tells not only what happened literally in Judea long ago, but also what can happen metaphysically anytime and anywhere to anyone who takes a mystical trip to the inner Bethlehem.

Actually, New Thought metaphysicians see the entire Bible as every person's story. "The Bible," declared Fillmore, "veils in its history the march of man from innocence and ignorance to a measure of sophistication and understanding." He viewed the Bible as one great parable illustrating the spiritual unfoldment of man. To him, not only the obviously mythical, legendary, and prophetic material in the Bible, but also the historical parts of both Testaments needed to be metaphysically interpreted because, as he went on to explain in the foreword to *Mysteries of Genesis,* "Over all hovers the divine idea of man, the perfect-man pattern, the Lord, who is a perpetual source of inspiration and power for every man. Those who seek to know this Lord and His manifestation, Jesus Christ, receive a certain spiritual quickening that opens the inner eye of the soul and they see beyond the land of shadows into the world of spirit."

In other words, even the historical material of the Bible means more than facts convey. For now, our concern is not whether the events of the Christmas story are factual. Important as facts may be, the greatest value of Bible stories lies in what the facts veil, what they symbolize or stand for. What the facts veil or symbolize are what Fillmore calls *divine ideas* or *Truth.* Our concern is the discovery of the divine ideas and Truth symbolized by the facts in the Christmas story.

Metaphysicians distinguish between fact and Truth. Facts are the situations, events, characters, places, and things that appear in life or in a story. Facts of a story are whatever an observer of the events might hear, see, taste, touch, smell, or otherwise experience. The facts of a story comprise its literal or surface meaning. Because what observers notice depends on their mental and emotional state and where they are in relation to an event, facts noticed or recorded by one person often differ from those noticed or recorded by another.

Beliefs about the actual physical world are considered facts, but, because change governs the actual physical world, such facts can change. To people of biblical times, the earth was the fixed, flat, middle zone of a three-layer universe with hell below and heaven above, around which the sun, moon, and stars moved. That is what their senses reported. That fact has changed radically.

Truth to the metaphysician is not relative and does not change. Truth refers to the invisible, eternal principles that underlie everything that appears in the outer world. Sometimes a fact coincides with Truth and may lead us to discover Truth, but Truth itself does not change. Truth endures.

In general, the word *metaphysics* refers to any system of thought by which people try to discover Truth. Because knowledge of the principles that give rise to or transcend the physical world gives human beings some degree of power over the environment, people of every known culture have searched for Truth. Spiritual metaphysics is the search for the Truth as it applies to humanity in relationship to the source of all that is and the total cosmic process—what is generally called God. Both aspects of the search for Truth and the discoveries are preserved in allegories, folktales, fables, legends, and—when Truth is primarily about humanity and the relationship between humanity and God—myths.

Myths are symbolic stories featuring characters, places, things, and actions that stand for or point to Truth and thus stimulate ideas "beyond the grasp of reason," to use the words of Carl Jung, the great Swiss psychologist. He also said that myths and the symbols in them "have not been invented consciously. They have happened."[1] They have arisen from what Jung called *the collective unconscious,* "the part of the psyche which retains and transmits the common psychological inheritance of mankind."[2]

Myths, then, are not fanciful tales composed to entertain, but serious attempts to explain or understand what cannot be explained or understood by reason alone. Some myths attempt to explain natural phenomena—from the creation of the universe to the behavior of animals and cycles of seasons; some tell how to deal effectively with nature and supernatural powers; some justify particular social customs; but the most important for the purpose of understanding the Christmas story are those that tell why people are as they are and how they can develop their own psychological or spiritual potential. As Joseph Campbell said, such myths are "metaphorical of spiritual potentiality in the human being" and are for "spiritual instruction."[3]

The latter kind of myth (and to some extent the former three) are what the depth psychologist Ira Progoff calls the "primary medium for intuitive insights into the ultimate nature of human existence."[4] The "ultimate nature," of course, is spiritual, and intuitive insights serve as a means of discovering the truth about ourselves as spiritual beings. If we choose to apply that truth in our daily lives, it can help heal those parts of our being that are wounded, release and integrate those parts we have repressed, help us to express heretofore unsuspected potential, and otherwise enable us to participate in our own evolution.

Ancient myths from widely separated parts of the world and dissimilar cultures are remarkably similar. Indeed, this similarity led to Jung's discovery of the collective unconscious. Fillmore recognized the collective unconscious, but he called it *race mind*.[5]

According to Jung, the collective unconscious consists of archetypes. Archetypes are innate, possible, and potential forms. We can think of them as energy patterns for functioning, perceiving, and conceptualizing that are common to all human beings. Each archetype may have positive and negative aspects, a light and a dark side, so to speak. Some archetypes have two or more (often three) phases appropriate to different phases of human life. In stories and dreams, archetypes are symbolized by gods, humans, animals, objects, and courses of action. In waking life, one might think of them as energy patterns which, when active in the psyche, may cause a person to behave, perceive, or conceptualize in ways common to all human beings. Fillmore would call them *divine ideas* because human beings come equipped with them and can express them variously.

To understand archetypes as energy patterns, the analogy of a children's dot-to-dot puzzle may be helpful. Imagine a square filled with dots or specks of energy, some of which are numbered. A child joins the numbered dots together in the correct sequence and discovers the outline of, let us say, a rabbit, which the child may then color to his taste. The connecting lines he draws and the colors he chooses will vary from the lines his sister draws and the colors she chooses. So it is with archetypes; no two individuals form and color or express any one archetype in the same way.

Archetypes are somewhat comparable to instincts because they have energy and will exert inner pressure toward outward expression. However, when we attain some degree of mature consciousness, we can often choose to allow or not allow some archetypes to determine our behavior.

Considered as a myth, the traditional Christmas story features the interplay of a number of archetypes. That does not mean the principal sources of the myth—the accounts of the birth of Jesus given in the New Testament—contain no facts at all. In the first place, according to Jung, archetypes are possible forms of human behavior and most of the characters in the story are human beings. In the second place, myths are often based on fact. Jesus was probably born in Palestine toward the end of Herod the Great's reign to parents named Mary and Joseph, who raised him in Nazareth.

Yet no one well-acquainted with worldwide mythology can miss the great similarity between the Gospel accounts of the life of Jesus (from conception to after the resurrection) and the stories about gods of many mystery religions of the ancient world. The early church fathers saw the similarity as indicating that in Jesus the ancient myths were realized. The similarity has led many scholars to conclude that Jesus did not exist.

But if Jesus did not exist, an incredible thing must have happened. Imagine that a committee of early first-century Jews (the 12 disciples) invented a messiah who did not resemble the kind of man they hoped could oust the hated Romans from their land. Next, they would have had to fabricate a biography out of myths not only from the religion of the Romans, but also from the religions of Egyptians, Greeks, and Syrians (to mention some they may have known), Hindus, Buddhists, and Chinese (with which they were not acquainted). Then they had to attribute to him many overlooked teachings from their own sacred

7

scriptures and ascribe to him such unpopular behavior as acceptance of women as equals, tolerance of non-Jews, friendship with "sinners," and forgiveness of Romans. They deliberately portrayed themselves as often being stupid or selfish and behaving shamefully. Then, to disseminate the entire fiction, they knowingly risked their lives; some even suffered death while steadily proclaiming faith in their lie. The entire scenario, including the fate of those who invented it, so appealed to Jews and Gentiles that, within a generation, the new religion attracted so many followers that Roman rulers felt threatened enough to persecute and martyr converts and committee members.

That is an incredible hypothesis. It is far more incredible than the likelihood that a remarkable man known as Jesus of Nazareth existed. In Jungian terms, Jesus was highly individuated; he expressed the higher Self to such an extent that his impact upon the minds and hearts of those who knew him brought to consciousness archetypes they projected upon him and then tried to integrate into their own psyches. That still goes on today among Christians and non-Christians to such an extent that Jung called Jesus Christ the "perfect symbol of the hidden immortal within the mortal man."[6] The "hidden immortal" is the archetype of the higher Self. When it becomes the active center of consciousness, it integrates and enriches all aspects of the psyche.

The basic assumption of this book is that the traditional Christmas story is based on one major fact, the fact that Jesus really did live; furthermore, it foretells metaphysically another fact, the fact that anyone can do as Jesus did and express the higher Self—the Christ or image of God.

Myths have foretold facts. For instance, the Genesis account of creation has features similar to the more ancient Assyro-Babylonian creation myth; but in the older myth, water is the primordial substance, while in the Genesis myth, the primordial substance is light. The biblical myth foretold a modern fact: Today the most knowledgeable scientists agree that the basic element (if it can be called that) of all matter is the photon, an infinitesimal fleck of light.

8

Interestingly, light is a recurring symbol for spirit and divine intelligence and wisdom. God is considered the primordial light, and Jesus, the archetype for the higher Self, was said in the Gospel of John to be "the true light that enlightens" everyone. Jesus exhorted His followers to let their light shine, in other words to let their spiritual selves—the image of God—express both within themselves and out into their world.

Understanding the metaphysical meanings in the traditional Christmas story can guide us on an inner, spiritual, or mystical trip to Bethlehem, where the Christ is born in consciousness to be the light that shines within us and radiates into our world. When understood metaphysically, the traditional Christmas story can serve as a guide to individual spiritual transformation.

Though the story begins six months before the child is conceived and closes when he is perhaps 4 years old, probably most of us are familiar with only selected parts—the announcement to Mary that she will bear God's son, the trip to Bethlehem, the birth in a stable, the visits of the shepherds, and the three wise men who followed the star, and perhaps the flight to Egypt to escape Herod's murderous wrath and the family's return to Nazareth after Herod's death. The entire traditional story contains much more, for it is a myth that illustrates the process by which anyone may allow the Christ to emerge as the ruler of consciousness. We discover the process only by approaching the traditional story as we approach any myth and, because each element in a myth symbolizes a potentiality or actuality within our own psyche, that approach involves metaphysical interpretation.

However, we need to know exactly what is meant by "the traditional Christmas story," and so it is retold in Chapter 3.

2

The Myth Is Created

For centuries, through prose, poetry, pageant, painting, sculpture, and song, people have retold the birth story of Jesus. They blended the only two Gospel accounts and added details that at first glance seem embellishments but that metaphysical interpretation shows are spiritually significant. The process began early, before the Gospels of Matthew and Luke were written. It may have begun when Gentile converts tried to understand how such a remarkable man as Jesus could be. There was an explanation handy in the pagan birth-myths of heroes and demigods— the union of a god and a mortal female produced a remarkable person.

The myth may have begun that way, or it may have begun when the impact of the man Jesus and his teachings stirred archetypes into action.

The writer of Mark was either unaware of the birth story or for some reason did not include it, because Mark's gospel, written about 70 CE, begins with the ministry of John the Baptist. The Gospel of John, written about 90 CE, also has no birth story; it begins with the spiritual significance of Jesus and then moves directly to the ministry of John the Baptist and the incident during which he declared himself the forerunner of the Lord.

The earliest mention of the birth of Jesus is in The Letter of Paul to the Romans, probably written in 56 or 57 CE. At the beginning of the letter, Paul identifies himself as a servant of Jesus Christ, "who was descended from David according to the flesh and designated Son of God in power according to the Spirit of holiness by his resurrection from the dead" (Romans 1:3-4). Since, according to the genealogies in Matthew (1:1-16) and Luke (3:23-38), Joseph, not Mary, was a descendant of David, Paul was saying, in effect, that Joseph sired Jesus. Paul knew that Jesus was special, but from his letters it is obvious that he wanted to encourage people to become like Jesus, a difficult assignment if Jesus did not have two human parents.

Paul met some of the original disciples, who undoubtedly shared whatever they knew about their Master. Perhaps no one told Paul anything about any unusual events connected with the birth of Jesus. Because people who have known any great person are eager to share all they know about the individual, it would be very strange for the disciples to withhold information that clearly showed the specialness of their hero. Perhaps they told him and he chose not to pass on the information. We do not know. We do know, however, that the virgin birth is essential to the metaphysical meaning of the Christmas story.

A long time passed between the birth of Jesus and the writing of the Gospel of Matthew, which has the first account of the birth. It was written in about 85 CE, more than 50 years after the crucifixion. Matthew mentions Mary's pregnancy by the Holy Spirit but implies that Jesus was born in a *house* (apparently Joseph's house) in Bethlehem. This account has the visit of wise men from the East, who followed a mysterious star that was seen by no one else. Only Matthew tells of Herod's killing of infants, the flight of the holy family to Egypt and, because according to the writer, Mary and Joseph originally lived in Bethlehem, the move to Nazareth.

The Gospel of Luke, written approximately 85 to 95 CE, is quite different. Luke has a prologue (included in the retelling of the story in the next chapter) that tells about the miraculous conception of John the Baptist as well as that of Jesus, then he tells about the census, the trip to Bethlehem, the birth in the stable, the visit of the shepherds, and, after all required ceremonies surrounding births have been performed in Jerusalem, the return to Nazareth.

The stories are not simply different, they are contradictory. Could it be that Jesus was born under ordinary circumstances either in Nazareth (as a few scholars believe) or Bethlehem (as both Matthew and Luke claim and tradition insists)? No one knows. At the time, births of common folk were not recorded, and apparently Jesus never said.

We are not even certain of the year when Jesus was born. At present, the most educated guess is sometime in 7 or 6 BCE on the assumption that, if the "slaughter of the innocents" (baby boys 2 years old and younger) did occur, Jesus had to have been born before Herod died in 4 BCE, if indeed that was the year of Herod's death. Historians are not certain of the date, some suggesting that it may have been as late as 2 or 1 BCE. But the Gospels of Matthew and Luke agree that Jesus was born toward the close of Herod's reign. Luke fixes the date by mentioning a world census. Unfortunately, that does not help because, according to the Jewish historian, Josephus, the census Luke mentions took place in 6 or 7 CE after the death of Herod.[1]

Some astronomers believe that the 7 BCE conjunction of Jupiter and Saturn that occurred in the constellation of Pisces, which astrologers of the time considered the "house of the Hebrew," may have been the origin of the legend of the star. In all probability, the author did not think stars are what astronomers have discovered them to be—gigantic, inanimate, swirling masses of energy, inconceivably far away from earth. To the ancients, stars were considered celestial entities, angel-like beings, and many passages in the Bible indicate the Jews shared that belief.[2] For instance, the Lord asks Job where he was when "the morning stars sang together" (Job 38:7), and Joel predicts that on the "day of the Lord ... the sun and the moon are darkened, and the stars withdraw their shining" (Joel 2:1-10). The prophet sees that something causes the sun and moon to darken, but the stars themselves withdraw their lights, as people would take away torches. So the Magi's star was an angel-like being that served as a guide who moved ahead of them (much as the "pillar of cloud" by day and the "pillar of fire" by night led Moses and the Hebrews through the wilderness of Egypt), waited for them when they rested, and descended to earth to point out the exact place where the child was to be found.

As to the season or month, there is no way of knowing. Matthew gives no hint of the time of year. Luke's inclusion of the shepherds in the field with the flock by night suggests any season except winter. To neither author was the month important. Oddly to modern Christians to whom Christmas is important, early Christians did not celebrate the birth of Jesus until about the third century, and then they celebrated three events—the visit of the wise men, John's baptism of Jesus, and the birth of Jesus—all on January 6. Nativity celebrations were not widespread until the fourth century when the church leaders chose December 25.

It was a wise and symbolic choice. From antiquity, on that date there was a winter solstice festival to celebrate the increase of light, the triumph of the sun over darkness. Former pagans could retain their festival but change the reason for it. The reason became the coming of the Sun of Righteousness prophesied by Malachi (4:2). The church leaders saw the birth of Jesus as fulfillment of the prophesy. Even a pagan custom, in itself a response to an archetype, contributed to the evolution of the Christmas myth.

About the same time, the ass, ox, and camels were included in a *bas-relief* of the nativity of a Christian sarcophagus.[3] Leading the camels are three wise men wearing caps like the one on a statue of Mithra, a Persian savior who was worshipped as the incarnation of eternal light and whose birthday was December 25 at midnight. The detail both echoes Matthew's intention to stress the universal significance of Jesus and identifies the wise men as Magi from Persia, information not given by Matthew. The date and time, the animals, the Persian visitors, all became permanent features in the Christmas myth. At Christmastime, we sing about the birth on a cold winter midnight and of the babe in a manger "where ox and ass are feeding," and we illustrate, erect, or enact nativity scenes that, like the fourth-century bas-relief, collapse time and depict the Magi and the shepherds present at the same time in the stable.

The confusion about dates indicates that though the stories are about a historical person, the actual or historical facts were not known. Furthermore, the writers were concerned with the meaning of Jesus' birth rather than with historical accuracy.

Through the centuries, when faith in the teachings of Jesus stirred the Christ archetype within them, people have responded by retelling the nativity story as they felt it should have happened or to convey symbolically what the birth of Jesus meant to them. Though, like the caps on the wise men, some additions symbolized purposes of early theologians, metaphysical interpretation uncovers more meaning in the symbols than the theologians, artists, or storytellers consciously intended.

Writings of early church leaders clearly indicate their recognition that the birth stories in Matthew and Luke could be disputed and so, like laypeople, they felt free to rework the Gospel material to convey the truth as they saw it. Indeed, that probably was the reason, though it may not have been conscious, that the canon included the two contradictory accounts. Each Gospel account by itself is incomplete; it points to only part of the Truth. But blended together, and with the additions that have been incorporated, the two form the traditional Christmas story that points to the Truth and so becomes a guide to transformation, a map for a transformative trip to a spiritual Bethlehem.

Now let us read the great myth that has evolved. It has been written in simple, contemporary language.

3

The Traditional (Blended) Christmas Story

In the final years that Herod the Great reigned as Rome's puppet king in Judea, some remarkable events occurred. They began when an angel appeared to a priest named Zechariah. He lived in a hill town of Judah with his wife, Elizabeth. They were childless and elderly. Zechariah had gone to Jerusalem for his annual two-week duty as a priest in the temple when, by lot, he was chosen to go alone to burn incense on the altar.

While the people outside prayed, he lit the incense. At that moment, an angel appeared, standing on the right side of the altar. The sight frightened the old man, but his fear changed to bewilderment when the angel said, "Do not be afraid, Zechariah, for your prayer is heard, and your wife Elizabeth will bear you a son, and you shall call his name John. And you will have joy and gladness, and many will rejoice at his birth ..."[1] The angel explained that John would be a prophet like Elijah, but his special mission would be to turn "the sons of Israel" back to God and help people prepare to receive the Lord.

When Zechariah protested that both he and his wife were too old, the angel reproved him, saying, "I am Gabriel, who stand in the presence of God; and I was sent to speak to you, and to bring you this good news." He added that, because Zechariah did not believe him, he would be unable to speak until after the child was born.

Outside, the people waited, wondering why the priest was so long at the altar, but when Zechariah came out and could not speak, they realized he must have had a vision. At the end of the two weeks, he returned to his home. Soon afterward, Elizabeth learned she was pregnant. For five months, she stayed in seclusion, giving thanks that God had taken away her barrenness.

In the sixth month of Elizabeth's pregnancy, God sent Gabriel to her kinswoman, Mary, who lived in Nazareth in Galilee. Mary was a virgin and betrothed to a man named Joseph, of the "house of David." Gabriel startled Mary with his greeting, "Hail, O favored one, the Lord is with you." Then he said, "Do not be afraid, Mary, for you have found favor with God. And behold, you will conceive in your womb and bear a son, and you shall call his name Jesus." He then told her that God would give her son the throne of David and he would rule over the "house of Jacob" forever.

Mary replied, "How shall this be, since I have no husband?"

The angel explained that the Holy Spirit would cause the miracle and the child would be holy, the Son of God. Then he told her that her aged kinswoman Elizabeth, who had been barren, was now six months pregnant with a son, because "with God nothing will be impossible."

Mary ceased arguing and said, "Behold, I am the handmaid of the Lord; let it be to me according to your word."

Gabriel disappeared.

In a few days, Mary hurried to visit her kinswoman. She entered Zechariah's house calling out to her cousin. When Elizabeth heard Mary's greeting, her baby moved within her and she was inspired to exclaim, "Blessed are you among women, and blessed is the fruit of your womb! And why is this granted me, that the mother of my Lord should come to me? For behold, when the voice of your greeting came to my ears, the babe in my womb leaped for joy. And blessed is she who believed that there would be a fulfilment of what was spoken to her from the Lord."

Mary replied with a prayer that praised God and expressed her complete acceptance of her task. She remained with Elizabeth for three months and returned to Nazareth just before Elizabeth had her baby.

When Elizabeth's baby was born, her neighbors and kinsfolk were very happy that God had taken away her barrenness. On the eighth day, the day when a baby boy was to be circumcised and named, the people thought the child should be named after his father, but Elizabeth said, "Not so; he shall be called John."

It was customary to name a child after someone in the family, and the people turned to Zechariah to ask him for the name. Zechariah asked for a tablet and wrote, "His name is John." At that moment, he regained his speech, and immediately blessed God. The people then realized that God had worked a miracle and the baby boy was special.

As for Zechariah, he was inspired and in a long prayer, he dedicated John to prepare the way for the Lord.

When Mary returned to Nazareth, Joseph realized that, though he and Mary were not yet married, she was pregnant. He was "a just man" and did not want to shame her, so, because in those days a betrothal was as binding as marriage, he decided to divorce her secretly. But in a dream, Gabriel appeared to him and said, "Joseph, son of David, do not fear to take Mary your wife, for that which is conceived in her is of the Holy Spirit; she will bear a son, and you shall call his name Jesus, for he will save his people from their sins." When he awoke, Joseph obeyed the angel. He married Mary, but he did not consummate the marriage until after the baby was born in Bethlehem.

Jesus was born in Bethlehem because Joseph had to travel to his tribal city to register in the first world census ordered by the Roman emperor Augustus. Bethlehem was the city of David's tribe, the one to which Joseph belonged. It was a four- or five-day journey from Nazareth to Bethlehem and Mary would soon have the child, so Joseph had her ride on an ass.

When Mary and Joseph arrived, Bethlehem was crowded. Though there was no room in the inn, the innkeeper, seeing Mary's condition, let them and the ass stay in the stable—a cave in the side of the hill where he kept his ox. Right away, the baby was born. Mary wrapped him in swaddling cloths and laid him in a manger.

That night, shepherds watching their flock in a nearby field were terrified and almost blinded by a great light. Then Gabriel appeared and said, "Be not afraid; for behold, I bring you good news of a great joy which will come to all the people; for to you is born this day in the city of David a Savior, who is Christ the Lord." The angel told them where to find the child, and then a heavenly choir joined him, saying, "Glory to God in the highest, and on earth peace among men with whom he is pleased!"

The angels disappeared, and the shepherds hurried to Bethlehem. They found Mary and Joseph and the babe in the manger. They knelt, presented their gift of a lamb, and reported what the angel had said. Mary was very quiet as she listened. As the shepherds returned to the fields, they glorified God for all they had seen and heard.

On the eighth day, the day of circumcision, Joseph obeyed the angel and named the child Jesus. The family moved to a house in Bethlehem where they could comfortably wait for the required two months to pass before they could go to the temple in Jerusalem and fulfill the Law of Moses with purification rites, the sacrifice of "a pair of turtledoves, or two young pigeons," and to dedicate Jesus to the Lord.

The day arrived. At the temple door, there was an old man named Simeon, a righteous and devout man who had had a revelation that he would not die until he had seen the promised savior of Israel. Inspired by the Holy Spirit, Simeon entered the temple; and when the parents brought in the child Jesus, he took the child in his arms and blessed God, saying, "Lord, now lettest thou thy servant depart in peace, according to thy word; for mine eyes have seen thy salvation which thou hast prepared in the presence of all peoples, a light for revelation to the Gentiles, and for glory to thy people Israel."

Then Simeon blessed the parents and said to Mary, "Behold, this child is set for the fall and rising of many in Israel, and for a sign that is spoken against (and a sword will pierce through your own soul also), that thoughts out of many hearts may be revealed."

A prophetess named Anna, the daughter of Phanuel of the tribe of Asher, was also there. She was an 84-year-old widow whose husband had died seven years after their marriage. Since then, she had remained in the temple, worshipping with fasting and prayer night and day. She joined Mary, Joseph, and Simeon and thanked God and spoke of God to everyone who was looking for the redemption of Jerusalem.

Following the ceremonies, the family went back to Bethlehem. Time passed. Then three Magi, wise men from the East, rode their camels into Jerusalem, asking people, "Where is he who has been born king of the Jews? For we have seen his star in the East, and have come to worship him." When word of them and their question reached Herod, he felt threatened. He called the chief priests and scribes together and asked them where the prophesied king would be born. They said, "In Bethlehem of Judea ..." and quoted the prophet Micah.

After the priests and scribes left, Herod secretly summoned the Magi. From them, he learned that they had first seen the star over a year before. Then he sent them to Bethlehem, saying, "Go and search diligently for the child, and when you have found him bring me word, that I too may come and worship him." Of course, that is not what Herod planned to do.

The star they had seen in the East led the Magi to the house where the baby was. With joy, they went into the house and when they saw Mary and her child, they bowed down to worship Him and gave their gifts of gold, frankincense, and myrrh. That night, they were warned in a dream not to go back to Herod, so they departed for their own country by a different route.

That same night, Gabriel appeared to Joseph in a dream and said, "Rise, take the child and his mother, and flee to Egypt, and remain there till I tell you; for Herod is about to search for the child, to destroy him." Joseph got up and put Mary and the baby on the ass and immediately started the journey to Egypt.

Herod was so furious when the Magi did not return to tell him exactly where the baby was that he had his troops kill all the male children in and around Bethlehem who were 2 years old or younger.

But Herod could not be sure that the special child had been killed, and the uncertainty made him almost mad and very ill. He died only a year or so after the murder of all those innocent children.

In Egypt, Gabriel visited Joseph in a dream once more to say, "Rise, take the child and his mother, and go to the land of Israel, for those who sought the child's life are dead." Joseph obeyed, but when the family reached Israel, he heard that Herod's son was the new ruler of Judea and he was afraid to go back to the house in Bethlehem. As a result of another warning dream, he took the child and Mary directly to Nazareth in Galilee.

That is the story that has evolved over the past 2,000 years. The following chapters are concerned not with historical accuracy, which cannot be ascertained, but with spiritual truth, which can be discovered. The story is approached reverently, as a sacred myth, which invites us to be transformed by participating in the spiritual process of rebirth. When the invitation is accepted, we consciously enter the kingdom of God, for as Jesus, the Christ child grown tall, said to Nicodemus, "... unless one is born anew, he cannot see the kingdom of God" (John 3:3).

The Metaphysical
Meaning

4

The Journey, Time, and Places

To psychologists, mythologists, and metaphysicians like Fillmore, elements of stories—whether biblical, mythological, folk, or fairy—as well as elements of dreams and fantasies symbolize elements of any human consciousness and all the stages, states, and processes through which consciousness moves. Thus each element of the Christmas myth symbolizes something that can or does exist or a process that can or does occur within us.

The Journey

The element that holds any story together and governs the selection of other elements is the theme, the central idea the story illustrates. The first indication of its theme is the actual framework of the Christmas story—a journey. A journey is an important mythic symbol for the process of transformation. The trip to Bethlehem is a round trip during which Mary and Joseph undergo a profound change; they leave Nazareth as a couple and, because the child is born while they are away, they return as a family. A newborn child is almost always the center of attention and the factor that transforms a couple into a family. The total journey in the Christmas story is archetypal for it illustrates the inner rebirth process through which the higher Self emerges as the center of consciousness, becomes the integrating force within it, and transforms the individual.

When and where events occur indicate the stage and state of consciousness favorable for a particular phase of the rebirth process.

The traditional Christmas story unfolds in Jerusalem, in a hill town in Judah, in Nazareth in Galilee, in Bethlehem when a world census was conducted, and in Egypt during the closing years of Herod the Great's reign as Rome's puppet king of Judea and most of the land of the Jews.

To understand the significance of the time, we first need to understand the metaphysical distinction between two important terms—*Israel* and *Jew*.

Israel. *Israel* is the name given to Jacob after he wrestled an angel until the angel blessed him. Among the meanings of the name are "contending or striving for God" and "dominion with God." Hebrews were called Israelites to signify their descent from Jacob and devotion to the one God. In the New Testament, references to Israel or the people of Israel symbolize a growing spiritual consciousness and an aggregation of thoughts governed by spiritual principle. Such thoughts are directly related to the realization of the omnipresence of God, which came to Jacob when, in the wilderness on his journey to find a wife, he had a dream in which God said, "Behold, I am with you and will keep you wherever you go ..." (Genesis 28:15). Awareness of the omnipresence of God is basic to the unfolding of spiritual consciousness.

Jew. Though the word *Jew* refers to a Hebrew, it specifically applies to a follower of Judaism, the religion founded on the Israel consciousness developed by Moses and contributed to by others over centuries. Like any religion, Judaism consists of definite beliefs, rules, and practices that govern the outer life of the community. Metaphysically, the word *Jew* or *Jews* symbolizes fixed religious thoughts or a consciousness governed by the determination to retain the beliefs, rules, and practices of Judaism. Such thoughts may or may not lead to spiritual consciousness.

The Time

The Christmas story takes place toward the end of the reign of Herod the Great when the Romans have ordered a world census.

Herod the Great. In the Christmas story, the time is metaphysical. It represents the stage of consciousness one must reach to begin the transformation process. It is symbolized by King Herod, who, though a historical person, is also an archetypal figure. Any king is a symbol for the ego. The ego is our personalized sense of our own identity. Though the ego rules consciousness and seems to have a life of its own, it is the product of our experience with the material environment. From birth through adolescence, we form our sense of self—our ego—primarily in response to other people's reactions to us and what we learn we must do to have our needs met and desires fulfilled so that we can fulfill our basic task—to survive. Experience leads us to believe we can safely express only certain aspects of ourselves, so the ego tries to choose which archetypes we will express and which we will repress.

Because King Herod had a long reign, he symbolizes a firmly established ego. The Christmas story unfolds within us when we have a well-established sense of identity of ourselves as individuals. The Christ, or higher Self, has infinite potential for expression. While we are in bodies, we are human and finite as well as spiritual and infinite, and our assignment is to transcend our sense of human identity to give individualized expression to the Christ. Apparently, it does not matter whether our sense of identity is admirable or not because the particular kind of ego symbolized by Herod is hardly admirable.

Ideally the ego or small self serves the greater, higher Self—the image of God—by giving individualized expression to the Self through a finite being. The ideal, however, is the goal of spiritual transformation. Until a person enters the transformation process, the ego revolves around its own concerns, and its primary concern is self-protection. Such an ego is called egocentric, and everyone is egocentric to some degree.

Herod represents a particular type of egocentric ego. The Jungian analyst, Fritz Kunkel, identified four basic egocentric types: "the clinging vine," which exerts power with childish, dependent behavior; "the star," which thrives on attention from other people; "the turtle," which tries to hide from the world; and "the Nero" or tyrant, which demands obedience.[1] Kunkel describes the tyrant ego as willful, harsh, selfish, and compassionless. Fillmore said that Herod represents "the ego in sense consciousness," which "does not understand man's true origin or the law of man's being" and is "narrow, jealous, destructive."[2] That is also an apt description of the tyrant ego. Herod symbolizes the egocentric ego in the tyrant mode. However, the other types of egocentric egos can be as tyrannical as the Herod type. Within us, they, too, try to destroy any threat to their rule.

Will Durant says that Herod was a man of "intellect without morals, ability without scruple, and courage without honor."[3] Herod was an Idumean—only technically a Jew. A century before his birth, his ancestors were forcibly converted, but Herod neither practiced nor believed in Judaism. He toadied to the Romans by building monuments to Augustus and other pagans, and he even built the magnificent temple in which the infant Jesus was dedicated to God, but Herod had only one god—himself.

He had 10 wives and 14 children and lived luxuriously but knew no happiness. To impress the world, he beautified Jerusalem and other cities of his realm with Greek-style buildings. To expand his power and protect himself, he acted ruthlessly. When he discovered conspiracies against him, he had the conspirators and their families tortured and killed. Even one of his own wives, three of his sons, and a mother-in-law were executed. This symbolizes that even what people most cherish may be destroyed by egocentricity.

Herod was called King of the Jews and ruled Judea, the name by which Rome designated the land or nation of Jews. A land or nation symbolizes a specific state of consciousness. Therefore, his rule represents egocentric domination over the state of consciousness formed by established religious beliefs and practices. It is metaphysically significant that Herod was not called King of Israel.

Herod ruled not by "divine right" but as a puppet of Rome. Rome was a materialistic society and capital of much of the world. Herod's rule represents the temporary, spurious rule of materialistic beliefs over religious thoughts. The world symbolizes total consciousness, and a capital represents the head or the intellect. Metaphysically, all the foregoing symbolizes that materialistic beliefs, which are foreign to the religious expression of spirituality, temporarily govern consciousness through egocentricity.

Significantly, the trip to Bethlehem occurs toward the end of Herod's life. Though the egocentric ego may rule a religiously oriented consciousness, it cannot rule a spiritually oriented one.

The ego of a spiritually conscious person is not egocentric, because that ego revolves around the higher Self. Spiritually oriented individuals may or may not be religious. They are concerned with their intimate, growing understanding of God; their inner relationship to God; and discernment and expression of God's will in their daily lives. There may or may not be a religion that supports their spiritual experience.

Any religion is a system of beliefs, rules, and practices that have grown out of someone else's spiritual understanding and experience. Though established to assist others to attain the same understanding and experience, the beliefs, rules, and practices are outer expressions and can be verbalized and adhered to without being internalized. As we are painfully aware, belonging to or even being a leader in a particular religious organization can serve egocentric purposes.

World Census. Metaphysically, the world is a state of consciousness formed by beliefs gained from experience with the material environment.

A census counts people. Because people symbolize thoughts and feelings, the world census symbolizes a time when all beliefs and feelings gained from the material environment are counted or called to account.

The Places

In the Bible, places symbolize states of consciousness. Events in the Christmas story shift from place to place. The first events occur in Jerusalem, then in a hill town in Judah near Jerusalem, and in Nazareth in Galilee. Later events occur in Bethlehem and Egypt.

Jerusalem. The very name gives its metaphysical meaning because, in Hebrew, *Jerusalem* means "habitation of peace." Since Jerusalem figures in the Christmas story three times, a peaceful state of mind is required for the spiritual processes symbolized by events set in that city.

Some facts about Jerusalem enrich the metaphysical meaning. The actual city sits on the edge of a ridge on the highest tableland in the country. Even today, people speak of "going up" to Jerusalem, for only from the south does a traveler descend to the city, and then the descent is only a few feet. That fact implies that peace of mind is a high state of consciousness that usually requires effort to reach. In addition, Jerusalem was a walled and fortified city. That fact implies that to maintain peace of mind one must protect and defend it.

Jerusalem was the center of government and, because the only temple was located there, of formal worship. Although much of Judaism was practiced within the home and the local synagogue, some rites could be performed only in the temple. Religious law required Jews to travel to Jerusalem to participate in those rites. Of the many possible metaphysical meanings in all those facts, the most important for us now is that (1) a peaceful state of consciousness is conducive to particular spiritual processes, and (2) though peace of mind is a high state of consciousness, it can be deceptive and dangerous because it can be ruled by a tyrannical egocentric ego (Herod the Great) that will build protective walls to retain the state of consciousness but nevertheless engage in destructive acts.

Hill Town in Judah. Zechariah and Elizabeth live in a hill town in Judah. *Judah* in Hebrew (Judea in Greek) means "praise of Jehovah" or "praise of God." Of course, a hill town is also a high place. Therefore, what is represented by the couple Zechariah and Elizabeth exists in the high state of consciousness formed by acknowledging and praising God. In such a high state of consciousness, which is present before the trip to Bethlehem takes place, the forerunner of the Christ is conceived and born.

Nazareth. Mary and Joseph lived in Nazareth of Galilee. In their day, Nazareth was a small, undistinguished, and obscure agricultural village of ordinary Jewish people. In Hebrew, Nazareth has several meanings; some are: branch, offshoot, sprout; also guarded, defended, and preserved. Though Nazareth was a Jewish village, Mary considered herself an Israelite (*Israel* means a "growing spiritual consciousness"). Combining the meanings of Nazareth and Israel gives the state of consciousness symbolized by the town. Nazareth symbolizes the state of consciousness that guards spiritual thoughts as they sprout and develop. Because Nazareth is a village of ordinary people, it represents an unsophisticated spiritual consciousness, not dependent on dogma and available to everyone.

Galilee. Nazareth is located in Galilee, a district of fertile hills, valleys, and fields and the great freshwater lake that still yields fish. It is a district that feeds people. The name *Galilee* literally means "rolling energy" or "momentum." Nazareth's location in Galilee suggests that as the Nazareth consciousness is nurtured, it grows and gains a momentum of its own.

It is in that state of consciousness that Mary receives and accepts her role in the Christmas story. To prepare herself, she goes to the hill town in Judah where she remains for about three months; after six months, she takes the trip to Bethlehem.

Bethlehem. Regardless of where Jesus was actually born, metaphysically speaking, the trip to Bethlehem is essential, not simply to fulfill the prophecy but because of the meaning of the name, the location, and character of the city, and its connection with David. *Bethlehem* literally means "house of bread or food, house of sustenance, house of living." Metaphysically, the city represents a consciousness of omnipresent substance or divine energy, which provides everything needed to create and sustain everything, including the emerging Christ.

Bethlehem is located in Judah, which we have seen symbolizes praise of God. Moreover, Bethlehem occupies a hill on the same tableland as

Jerusalem, but, being to the south, the way between it and Jerusalem is, at points, on a slightly higher elevation. So Bethlehem is one of the few places where the traveler goes up rather than down from Jerusalem. It is the most convenient route for the Magi to have taken when they left Herod. The geographical location has a metaphysical meaning: We must rise for a while a little above peace of mind to reach the state of consciousness where we find the Christ within ourselves.

Significantly, Bethlehem, a city of common folk, had no walls. Metaphysically, that implies that anyone can enter the consciousness of omnipresent substance. It needs no protective walls to isolate or defend it.

Luke called Bethlehem "the city of David" because David's family lived there. Bethlehem was the center for the tribe of Benjamin. *Benjamin* means "son of good fortune." Metaphysically, the tribe symbolizes faith, for through faith in God, good fortune comes. The name *David* means "beloved, loved, well-beloved." Metaphysically, David represents divine love (God as love), not fully developed but at least individualized in human consciousness.

Any city represents a state of consciousness; any king represents ego; and David was a king. So as the city of David, Bethlehem represents a state of consciousness dominated by faith and ruled by love. Only in such a consciousness can the Christ be born and become the ruling factor within the psyche, because only in such a consciousness does the ego (the ruling will and sense of identity) begin to revolve around the higher Self.

Egypt. Meanings for the Hebrew name for Egypt that apply to the story are "shut-in" or "restraint." Egypt is a traditional symbol for both man's animal nature or material body and the lower mental plane that knows about things of the world and has worldly desires. The body does impose restraints upon the spiritual nature and, metaphysically speaking, restraint is needed to protect the emerging Christ until the tyrannical egocentric ego can no longer harm it. Moreover, on earth the spiritual image of God occupies a material body; its first task is to survive long enough to unfold the image, and that requires knowledge of things of the world. In addition, development of the whole person requires understanding of worldly desires and their proper function in spiritual development. The flight to Egypt and the small family's stay there, therefore, symbolize the part of the transformation process during which the new idea of the Christ is hidden until it is firmly established in consciousness and can illuminate knowledge and understanding of worldly things and desires.

5

The Symbols

In presenting the metaphysical meanings of the theme and setting of the Christmas story, information was given about how those meanings could have arisen. The same method is used in this chapter on the general symbolism of male and female characters and the specific symbolism of animals, numbers, and things. Such information can aid in understanding and interpreting any symbolic material, whether in our own dreams and waking fantasies or in fairy tales, fables, legends, and myths from any culture, the Bible, or even actual life.

Yes, life can be metaphysically interpreted. Every word or act is symbolic because each translates something that cannot be heard or seen into perceptible sound and movement. That something is the thought or feeling that is expressed through words and acts. So knowing fundamentals of metaphysical interpretation helps us gain greater understanding of ourselves, other people, and the events of life from the most mundane to the most unusual.

The writers of both the Hebrew and the Christian scriptures saw symbolism in everything about them. They believed that aspects of God are expressed through all creation. They believed that God communicates with humanity through history, showing what does or does not fulfill the divine plan for creation, what will or will not contribute to human happiness and spiritual growth. They believed each human being is designed to express the image of God. Despite the fact that they called God *Father*, they saw each person as potentially whole, endowed with all aspects of the divine image. God, of course, being bodiless has no gender, but God's image manifests as male or female. A man tends to favor expression of aspects of God that differ from those expressed by a woman. Thus, not only do biblical characters portray themselves but they also represent traits associated with their sex.

In world literature, human traits considered essentially masculine or feminine are remarkably similar to those of biblical men and women. They are archetypal.

The characters of the Christmas story represent archetypes and other aspects of total human nature, two of which are thinking and feeling. Thinking expresses certain aspects of God; feeling expresses other aspects of God. Because the story focuses upon Mary, the aspects that are traditionally associated with the feminine nature or principle are given first.

Feminine Attributes

The Soul. The feminine principle is considered passive and receptive, and therefore, a woman represents the soul—the form, so to speak, that gives shape to the spiritual essence that God breathes into the God-image at the beginning of creation. Fillmore and Jung agree that the soul (to psychologists the *psyche)* is our total consciousness—conscious and subconscious or unconscious. The soul comprises all that it receives from Spirit and all that it acquires from experience with the material world. Although in his Bible interpretation system, Fillmore saw women characters as symbols for the soul, he recognized the soul has no gender. In his system, men symbolize the thinking phase of the soul and women symbolize its emotional or feeling phase.

Matter. Woman also represents matter, presumably because, like the soul, matter is a form filled by the formless. The words *matter* and *mother* have a common Latin root, suggesting the archetypal origin of this association.[1]

Intuition. The soul is recognized as the spiritual part of ourselves. Because communication is best between like beings, woman represents intuition, which is the ability to receive both direct communication from God and messages from other souls without the intermediary of speech.

Wisdom. As chapter after chapter of the Book of Proverbs and the statues before law courts indicate, wisdom is considered feminine. Wisdom is the ability to discern intuitively the best or most godlike way to make use of knowledge and to judge on the basis of principle righteously and impartially, as God judges.

Love. "God is love," declared the writer of the First Letter of John (4:8). The writer was not referring to the grand emotion but to the principle of oneness that harmonizes all creation. So because woman represents the soul, which is spiritual and therefore one with God, she also is a symbol for love.

Relatedness. Ideally, love as the principle of oneness should govern all relationships. Thus, woman represents the ability to relate harmoniously to God, other people, and the material environment.

Nurture. Woman also represents the nurturing ability, an obvious association with her prolonged role in reproduction.

Inner Life. All the above indicates that the feminine principle governs the inner life of the individual.

Feeling Nature. Since feelings are inner experiences, in the Bible, whether a female character is as innocent and obedient as Mary or as sophisticated and willful as Jezebel, she represents one or more of the feminine aspects of God and something about the feeling nature of any man or woman. Of course, any aspect may be expressed positively or negatively.

Masculine Attributes

The Spirit. The Hebrew word for *Spirit* ("ruach") used in the creation account in Genesis 1:2 is "feminine in form," but in most myths, Spirit is represented by a male figure.[2] Perhaps that is because in most cultures, men initiate new activities. Whatever the reason, Spirit is considered masculine.

Power. Spirit is the source of power that makes activity possible, so the masculine principle is power. A man represents power active in the outer world.

Creativity. Spirit creates all things in the cosmos, so man represents the ability to form and shape material things.

Intellect. Spirit is divine mind or intelligence, so man represents the intellect. The intellect enables us to gather and store knowledge for use primarily in the outer material realm.

Reason. Spirit is the source of order, and reasoning is an orderly activity of the intellect, so man represents reason. Reason is the ability to process knowledge, to analyze, to connect ideas and facts, and differentiate between cause and effect. The ability to reason is the principal tool human beings use to manage the outer world.

Protection. Spirit protects creation, so man represents protection. This is an obvious association with the masculine role in almost any society.

Outer Life. All the above indicates that the masculine principle governs the outer life of the individual.

Thinking Nature. Since thinking is humanity's primary tool for dealing with the outer world, in the Bible, a male character—with the exception of Jesus, who demonstrates the Christ or whole image of God— represents one or more of the masculine aspects of God and something positive or negative about the thinking nature of any man or woman.

Human beings exhibit, to some extent, all the attributes associated with either sex. Whether male or female, each is a threefold being, spirit-soul-body. Women think, men feel, and either can be wise, creative, nurturing, or protective. So it is in the Bible; many of the men and women were real people who exhibited some attributes of the opposite sex, but each can also be seen to represent specific aspects of God associated with his or her gender.

Some human traits, however, are not specifically associated with either gender. Those that seem to be acquired through experience with the material world, rather than through divine inheritance, are sometimes symbolized by animals.

Animals

From a Jungian standpoint, an animal is an archetypal symbol of some aspect of the instinctual nature and, depending on the context, may be viewed as positive or negative. Occasionally, however, an animal may symbolize the external or physical expression of a spiritual attribute that may or may not be associated with gender.

More animals appear in the Christmas story as we tell it than in the Gospels from which it arose. Matthew mentions no animals; Luke implies sheep with the word "flock" and specifically mentions the offering of "a pair of turtledoves or two young pigeons," although he does not say which were offered. Over time, theology and tradition added a lamb (which, though an immature sheep, has a distinctive symbolic meaning), ass, ox, and camels.

Ass. A traditional symbol of stubbornness, persistence, and endurance, the ass also represents humility and courage, which are traits expressed by the so-called lower nature of human beings. Because the lower nature is formed by experience with the external world, it is associated with the body. When an ass is being ridden, it may symbolize the body because it is carrying and being controlled by whatever the rider represents, just as our visible body carries and is controlled by our invisible consciousness. St. Francis of Assisi apparently made this association, for he called his body *Brother Ass*.

The ass is also a symbol for Set, the ancient Egyptian god of darkness, ignorance, limitation, and negation, so it is an appropriate symbol for what Jung calls the *shadow*, the combined tendencies and attributes (positive or negative) that an individual has rejected or repressed.

Ox. The ox, a castrated bull, is a symbol for Set's brother, Osiris. Osiris was the ancient Egyptian god of light, intelligence, creativity, and life who brought cosmic or spiritual forces and power into the material world. Osiris was slain by his jealous brother, Set, but was restored to life by Isis. So theologians' inclusion of the ox symbolized a new infusion of cosmic or spiritual forces and power and the triumph of the Christ over the resurrected god of the Egyptians.

Scholars also believe that early theologians probably included the ass and ox in nativity scenes to imply that the Christ reconciles opposites.

In traditional symbolism, the ox also represents some positive human tendencies—self-sacrifice, patient labor, productive energy, and submission to authority.

Camel. As the chief means of desert transportation over great distances, camels were added to indicate that the wise men had traveled far, all the way from Persia, to pay homage to the Christ.

A camel symbolizes strength, endurance, and perseverance. The negative attributes it may represent are rudeness, stupidity, and a bad temper.

Lamb. A lamb symbolizes purity, innocence, sweetness, and forgiveness, and thus harmlessness. Since these spiritual qualities are represented by an animal, the lamb represents the potential for them that is hidden in human nature. Of course, the lamb also symbolizes meekness and sacrifice and specifically points to the manner in which Jesus went to the crucifixion. Weakness and dependence are the only negative attributes it represents.

Sheep. A flock of sheep represents the aggregate of the most valuable human attributes that have evolved from the lower nature, attributes which, because they also express our true nature, are called the seven virtues and usually identified as honesty, prudence, temperance, courage, justice, charity, and compassion. Exercise of the virtues makes community living possible, predictable, and pleasant. Sheep, of course, do not display any of those virtues, but perhaps because of the great value of sheep in ancient societies, they were deemed appropriate symbols. To the Jews, sheep were a source of wealth, not because of the meat but the wool.

Sheep were carefully tended, fed well, nursed when sick or wounded, sought when lost, and kept alive for as long as possible to provide wool and the income it brought for their owners. For that reason, the offering of a lamb or a sheep as either a gift or sacrifice was a great act of faith, a sign of trust in God to replace the offering. As a negative symbol, sheep represent blind obedience.

Turtledove. The turtledove, which is a distinct variety of dove, is an ancient symbol for fidelity and human affection. It may also represent the negative trait of timidity.

Pigeon. Because originally a young dove was called a pigeon, symbolic meanings of the dove apply to the pigeon. In pagan religious symbology, the dove had many meanings, some of which are much the same in the Bible. In both the Hebrew and Christian scriptures, it represents purity, gentleness, peace, and aspiration. It is also a symbol for the soul and for the Holy Spirit, the Spirit of God active within creation. There are no negative attributes associated with the dove. As we can see, animals are not mere embellishments to the Christmas story; they are archetypes and are metaphysically significant.

Numbers

Numbers in the Christmas story are also significant. The mystical meanings attached to them are so ancient, widespread, and similar that the meanings appear to be archetypal, to preexist in the collective unconscious rather than to originate solely from experience with the material world.

Two. Depending upon context, two may symbolize reflection, opposition, duality, polarity, or equilibrium. One stands for spiritual essence, God, beingness itself. In the creative act, God produces two, retaining the oneness of the creator but reflecting it in some manner in what is created. From the Jungian standpoint, the number two represents that something is coming into consciousness.

Three. Three symbolizes spiritual synthesis. The Holy Trinity—Father, Son, and Holy Spirit—expresses the Christian concept of the one and only God. Human beings are a synthesis of three—spirit-soul-body. Three also stands for the completeness of some inner spiritual process and the process of creation and manifestation—mind-idea-expression. This number is also a symbol for creative masculinity.

Five. Five represents the idea of the human being. The body has four limbs and the head that controls them, and the human hand has four fingers and the thumb, which makes possible participation in the creative process. We also have five senses through which we experience the outer world.

Six. Six symbolizes perfection and harmony. It is also the numerical symbol for the human soul, a meaning that is at least as old as and probably older than Genesis. According to the writer of that book, on the sixth day, God made man and "breathed into his nostrils the breath of life; and man became a living being." The soul is the essence of God that gives us life. A six-pointed star composed of two equilateral triangles—the apex of one pointing upward and the apex of the other pointing downward—symbolically signifies the descent of spirit into matter and represents the soul. Because the soul is of the same essence as God-Spirit, it is pure; therefore, six also symbolizes purity and virginity.

Seven. Seven stands for perfect order and the completion of a cycle in the material world. A week comprises seven days, the spectrum seven basic colors, and the musical scale seven basic notes. Seven symbolizes completion of a process in the soul. Seven also has a moral significance.

There are seven basic sins and seven basic virtues. In addition, seven is a symbol for wisdom.

Eight. Because it follows seven, eight stands for entrance into a new condition or cycle. Eight is a symbol for regeneration and for rebirth. Laid on its side, the numeral 8 represents eternity.

Eighty-Four. Eighty-four is the exact age given for the prophetess, Anna, who was present at the dedication of the infant Jesus in the temple. To understand the significance of 84 requires knowing the symbolism of 12, because in numerology 84 reduces to 12 (8 + 4 = 12) and seven multiplied by 12 yields 84.

Twelve. Twelve stands for salvation and for holiness. It symbolizes cosmic order's harmonization of spiritual and material cycles. In ancient times, the heavens were considered the abode of God and the 12 signs of the Zodiac governed the 12 months of the year. The word *twelve* appears 167 times in the Bible as the specific number of, for instance, rods, stones, wells, fountains, oxen, cities, tribes, years, disciples, baskets of scraps, angels, and gates. It always signals that the items are important symbols. Twelve is also frequently hidden in larger numbers as it is in 84.

Combine the meanings of seven and 12, and 84 signifies the emergence of cosmic or spiritual order following the completion or fulfillment of required cycles of human experience.

Numbers in the Christmas story enhance its total meaning. So do things. They symbolize important elements of our total being and refer to parts of the spiritual process illustrated by the story.

Things

Temple. A temple or any other building dedicated to worship is deliberately designed to symbolize basic beliefs, one of which is that a deity resides within the structure. The temple in Jerusalem (whether built by Solomon or Herod) was designed to symbolize the cosmos as the Jews pictured it. Jesus used the temple as a symbol for his human body. So to Christian metaphysicians, the temple symbolizes the body, regenerated or glorified by spiritualized consciousness, in which the Spirit of God resides.

Altar. The altar is the focal point of the temple where devotion to God is expressed in conscious communication with God through prayer and, in ancient times, through sacrifice. The altar represents the spiritual center of consciousness where one expresses love for God, consciously communes with God, and gives up the lower for the higher Self or the personal for the spiritual life.

Right Side. The right side of anything symbolizes the stirring of the positive, outgoing principle of action or energy, while the left side represents passivity or incoming energy.

Star. Because stars (whether considered living beings or inanimate objects) are in the heavens (thought by the ancients to be the abode of God), they symbolize ideas that come from God rather than from the process of human reasoning, so any star stands for a Truth. The star that guided the wise men to Bethlehem to find the Christ has a special meaning. It symbolizes both the idea of the indwelling Christ and the power of that idea to lead us to its realization. In other words, the star signifies the compelling conviction of the Christ idea. It may also symbolize spiritual aspiration. It is significant that in the story no one but the Magi, or wise men, see the star.

East. As a direction, the East is an abstraction, for it is always relative to where one is at in the moment. Because the sun, the source of life-giving light, rises in the East, it is an enduring symbol of God, the giver of life and the primordial light. When used symbolically, the word is generally capitalized. So in the Christmas story, the East signifies the inner spiritual realm.

Swaddling Cloths. Newborn babies were wrapped or swaddled in long bands of cloth to protect them from the cold and to brace their bodies to protect them from injury. Swaddling cloths indicate helplessness and symbolize protection and necessary restraint or limitation.

Crowded Inn. Any dwelling place represents a state of consciousness. An inn is a place where a number of people, men and women, may for a price have temporary shelter. In the Christmas story, people from many areas speaking various dialects and languages would be in any inn in Bethlehem. Though most would have come because of a tribal connection with the city of David, some would have been foreigners in Bethlehem for other reasons. Men represent thoughts, women feelings. The crowded inn of the Christmas story symbolizes a temporary state of consciousness in which thoughts and feelings are mixed and confused. Moreover, there is a price to pay for staying in such a state.

Cave. Because the stables of Bethlehem were caves, the symbolism of a cave applies to the Christmas myth. Prehistoric man used caves for religious rites, a practice that survived into historic times. Followers of mystery religions conducted ceremonies in caves. Meetings of gods were thought to occur in caves. A cave symbolizes the sacred and the mysterious.

Since a cave is a dark, concealed place in the earth once associated with the Great Mother Goddess, it is a womb symbol. In Jungian psychology, the cave represents the collective unconscious.

Manger. A container for food for domestic animals, a manger symbolizes provision for the human being in which the Christ consciousness becomes manifest.

Night. Night is a symbol of the collective unconscious, potentiality, and germination.

Light. Light is a universal symbol for Spirit, intellect, and wisdom. It also represents morality and the seven virtues, since they are godlike human attributes.

House. A house represents the usual state of consciousness suggested by the owner's or inhabitant's sex, name, and other particulars. Just as a person may change residence, one may change consciousness. The word *house* was used to refer to ancestry as in "the house and lineage of David." Metaphysically understood, the expression implies the same kind of consciousness as David exhibited.

Gold. An obvious symbol for enduring wealth, gold represented to Fillmore "spiritual gifts; the riches of Spirit" and the "consciousness of the omnipresent richness of substance."[3] Substance is the spiritual essence of which all things are made. The Christ endows us with such a consciousness. Another symbolic meaning for gold is spiritual wisdom.

Incense. Actual burning of incense releases the energy from a solid into heat and smoke, so the process represents transmutation—an almost instantaneous change from a slower to a faster vibration or lower to higher state of being. Even after the smoke has become invisible, incense is detectable. So incense also symbolizes both the presence of Spirit or God and silent prayer—inner communication with God that raises consciousness and produces detectable outer changes. Almost every known religion features the burning of something as a religious rite.

Frankincense. Frankincense, an aromatic resin from a tree not native to Palestine or Persia, had to be imported and was therefore expensive and valuable. Because it was the only incense burned on the altar of the temple in Jerusalem, frankincense is a symbol for holiness or purity, the presence of God, and the potential for transmutation. Transmutation is the process by which consciousness changes its orientation from focusing upon the material world to focusing upon spiritual concerns.

Myrrh. Myrrh, also an aromatic resin, was used in ointments and perfumes and for embalming. Because of its association with perfume, it is a symbol for the attracting power of love, peace, and bliss. Because of its use for embalming, it symbolizes the eternality of Spirit and, in the Christmas story, because the Christ is the eternal, indestructible image of God, the gift of myrrh foreshadows the resurrection. We will now consider the characters in the Christmas story.

6

The Characters

There is ample evidence that biblical material is intended to convey more than its literal meaning. Much evidence is supplied by proper names, whether of places or persons. We have already seen that place names in the Christmas story can symbolize states of consciousness. That is because it was customary to name a place to suggest its nature or commemorate significant events that occurred there.

Names of persons can also symbolize states of consciousness or active factors in consciousness or any archetypal possibility or potentiality—all available to any human being. Because the ancient Hebrews believed that the sound and meaning of a name influenced the nature of the individual and other people, they named their children carefully. They believed names to be so important that when a person went through a profound change of consciousness, God gave him or her a new name. For instance, when God made the covenant with Abram, God changed his name to Abraham and changed his wife's name from Sarai to Sarah. The Hebrew meaning of *Abram* is "father of exaltation," but the meaning of *Abraham* is "father of a multitude." The meaning of *Sarai* is "bitter" or "contentious," but the meaning of *Sarah* is "princess" or "noble woman." In the Christmas story, names for the two infants are so important that they are determined not by their parents but by God—John and Jesus.

The symbolism of the characters and the meanings of names tell us much about how to prepare for and then make our transformative trip to our spiritual Bethlehem. Named characters are presented in the order of their appearance in the story, not the order of their importance, for the order of appearance itself is symbolic of the total process.

Names and Characters

Angels. Whether or not angels are a higher order of entities, angels symbolize messages from God. Although not human beings, angels are important characters in the Christmas story and in the spiritual process it symbolizes. In one form or another, angels or angel-like entities appear as messengers from the spiritual realm in myths of widely different cultures and even in sophisticated, esoteric philosophical systems. We may, therefore, consider them symbols for the archetype of communication with the spiritual source of being, no matter what the source is deemed to be. Angels may appear in anthropomorphic or fantastic form, but their function is always to reveal some aspect of divine will.

Interestingly, although angels appear in the Christmas story, they figure hardly at all in the rest of the biography of Jesus. Angels minister to Jesus following the 40 days in the wilderness, and he refers to angels several times during his teachings, but at no time does a gospel writer indicate that God communicated with Jesus through an angel. Angels reenter the gospels to speak to human characters only after the crucifixion. Since Jesus demonstrated the whole image of God, the higher Self in us, the implication is clear—a consciousness integrated by the higher Self and expressing it has no need for an intermediary between it and God. Such a consciousness, as Jesus taught, is always aware that it is one with the spiritual source, "the Father."

Gabriel. Luke identified the angel of the Lord who appeared to Zechariah and Mary by this name, which means "mighty man of God" or "God is my strength." In the Christmas story, the angel Gabriel symbolizes the wisdom of allowing the Christ nature to emerge and integrate all aspects of consciousness. The active inner Christ has power over outer material conditions. It makes one mighty, so to speak.

Though Luke says only that an angel of the Lord appeared to the shepherds, and Matthew does not name the one who spoke to Joseph, in dramatizations of the traditional Christmas story, Gabriel is God's messenger to all characters. That Gabriel should be the sole messenger is psychologically and spiritually appropriate, for each character represents some aspect of consciousness empowered by God.

Priest. A priest is a male who is authorized to perform religious rites. Anthropological and archaeological studies indicate that prehistoric human groups had specific religious rites. A rite expressing belief in a deity indicates the presence of a religion. Any religion consists of traditional beliefs about the relationship between a deity and humanity. The conclusion of most anthropologists is that religious tendencies are innate. A priest is a male, so a priest symbolizes the intellectual control of natural religious tendencies. A priest, then, is an archetypal figure that represents a consciousness governed by tradition.

Zechariah. The name means "whom Jah (Jehovah, God, the Lord) has remembered" or "the Lord is remembered." Zechariah, the father of John the Baptist, was an old priest when Gabriel appeared to him. At the beginning of the story, he represents the archetype of the priest—a well-established, tradition-bound thinking nature devoted to fulfilling the proper forms of worship. The meaning of the symbol then changes to suggest a consciousness in transition from intellectual understanding to spiritual understanding. He is in the process of spiritual awakening, of becoming conscious of the things of Spirit that underlie the forms of religion.

Elizabeth. The name means "God's oath." A woman symbolizes love (the principle of oneness) and represents the archetype of the soul. As the wife of Zechariah, Elizabeth symbolizes a consciousness in which love and confidence in God's promises or oaths are united with intellectual understanding during the process of transition. She, therefore, represents a disciplined soul and feeling nature.

At the beginning, Elizabeth was "advanced in years," married but barren. So she also represents the archetype of the mother, a form or potentiality not yet given substance. Although the soul is, figuratively, the mother of the Christ, it must first attain the phase conducive to conceiving and manifesting attributes represented by John the Baptist, and a mature, disciplined soul is in that phase. Elizabeth, then, symbolizes a phase of soul unfoldment that precedes the emergence of the Christ.

John. The son of Elizabeth and Zechariah, known as John the Baptist and destined to be the forerunner of the Lord, represents the thinking nature at work to prepare consciousness for the rule of the Christ.

John, the name bestowed by God, has several meanings, but those most applicable to the forerunner of the Christ are "grace and mercy of the Lord," "meekness," "fertility," and "love." Grace is the infinite, eternal love and mercy of God that are always active, whether or not human beings are deserving. To many people, the emergence in consciousness of John the Baptist is often as irrational and unexpected as the conception of a child by a barren woman; they have done nothing to attain the state. John represents both conscience or the moral nature and a high intellectual perception of Truth. Fillmore saw the mature John as representing the illumined intellect, which reasons its way to Truth.

Conscience is concerned with right conduct between human beings, so John symbolizes the archetype of the judge. When conscience emerges or the judge becomes active, it often stops people from continuing a course that would harm or deprive others. A sudden intellectual perception of Truth, such as the importance and value of individuals or the abiding presence of God, can burst upon the consciousness seemingly from nowhere.

John also represents meekness. Meekness is teachability and tractability, the kind demonstrated by domesticated animals. The grown-up Baptist wore animal skins and was a fiery speaker but was himself disciplined by his understanding of the Law. He was meek enough to understand that he was not the Master, only the forerunner.

He had a great following; crowds came to be purified by baptism. He represents the fertility of the moral nature and intellectual perception of Truth, particularly the idea of purification. When activated, the moral nature tends to permeate consciousness. One perception of Truth tends to lead to another and another. Purification of any aspect of consciousness tends to have an effect on other aspects.

47

John's devotion to principle, even though it cost him his life, symbolizes love in the masculine mode.

It is significant that John's mother and Mary were cousins and thus John and Jesus were related. The moral nature and illumined intellect are closely related to the Christ.

Child. In general, a child symbolizes a fresh but undeveloped idea, a potentiality, the future, and new life. There are two children in the Christmas story. Because both are conceived as a result of God's will, both represent the archetype of the divine child, the child born to fulfill a specific, assigned mission as well as all that any child symbolizes.

The infant John, being born of human parents—but only because of God's power to overcome barrenness—represents a child-hero aspect of the archetype of the divine child, one whose nature is human but raised almost to divinity, to more power than the human being usually possesses. All that John represents is already active to some extent in existing consciousness. But his birth symbolizes the infusion of new life into those ideas.

The infant Jesus, born of a human virgin and sired by the Holy Spirit, represents a god-like child, one whose nature is, in the words of the church fathers, "fully human and fully divine." His birth symbolizes a brand-new idea, the integration of all that is human and all that is divine within the soul. The birth of either aspect of the archetype signifies that the inner process leading to wholeness has begun. Jungian psychologists call this process "individuation," and Fillmore calls it spiritual evolution.

Mary. Mary, the central character in the traditional Christmas story, represents the archetype of the pure or purified soul. Her readiness to bear the holy child symbolizes the pure soul's readiness to allow the full expression of the Christ. The story tells in symbols how the soul prepares for and participates in that process. Mary is, therefore, a complex symbol.

Of course, she also represents the feeling nature functioning in the most positive ways. Because Gabriel appears to her directly rather than in a dream, she represents intuition functioning as it is designed to function, as the conscious connection with God-Mind.

Among the meanings of her name, the one that applies most in the Christmas story is "myrrh," which symbolizes love and the eternality of spirit. As the mother of Jesus, Mary symbolizes love in its highest sense. The love she symbolizes is the idea of eternal spiritual harmony with everyone and everything and the soul's eternal oneness with God.

Mary is young. Youth always suggests vitality and as yet unrealized possibilities. Thus, Mary symbolizes the soul's eternal vitality and infinite possibilities. She is a virgin. Virginity symbolizes purity, so she represents the pure or purified soul. Because the Virgin itself is an archetype for the original soul, which is neither feminine nor masculine but both—in other words, hermaphroditic—Mary also represents the archetype of the original soul, one not adulterated with duality or error of any kind.

Joseph. The name means "whom Jehovah will add to" and "he shall increase progressively." Being male, Joseph symbolizes all aspects of the thinking nature. His name signifies that the process of evolution enhances conscious awareness of Spirit by enriching all aspects of the masculine part of the total nature. Joseph is of the "house and lineage of David." David represents divine love individualized in human consciousness, so Joseph represents human awareness of spiritual oneness. Because he hears and responds to angelic messages, he also symbolizes wisdom. Of course, he represents the positive aspects of the father archetype— nurturer, provider, and protector.

Jesus. Jesus is the Greek translation of the Hebrew name Jeshua or Joshua and means "whose help Jehovah is; deliverance; safety; salvation; savior; deliverer; helper; prosperer; deliverance through Jehovah." Though the grown-up Jesus demonstrated all meanings of the name, he taught that it is the Christ, the image of God or the higher Self, that helps, prospers, delivers, and saves, not the man who demonstrated the power of the Christ in human form.

49

As the unborn child of the Holy Spirit, he symbolizes the divine idea of the image of God latent in every soul—the suspicion, we might say, that there is something divine about us. When that suspicion arises, the process of transformation is about to begin. Significantly, that process is not dependent upon any material event, symbolized by Mary's virginity. It is begun by spirit, not by man.

As the newborn child, Jesus represents the archetype of the divine child who has the power to activate all parts of consciousness. When this archetype emerges into a consciousness that is not ready to accept it, the egocentric ego feels threatened and often tries to repress it. Not surprisingly, many myths of the divine child involve a threat to the child's life.

A newborn child is helpless and fragile, needing the cooperation of both parents to survive. So the newborn Jesus symbolizes the integrating factor that brings the thinking and feeling natures into cooperation for the process of spiritual evolution.

Shepherds. Luke implies that the shepherds in the Christmas story owned the flock they watched, since he calls it "their" flock. That they leave their flock (their wealth) untended to find the child clearly indicates the symbolic nature of the episode. The shepherds represent the forces within us that protect and guard the valuable human virtues represented by sheep. They also represent thoughts that are faithful to God. That the shepherds are common folk who are at work in the fields by night signifies that the forces are present in the unconscious of everyone, for darkness or night is a frequent symbol for the unconscious phase of mind. In other words, the shepherds represent the archetype of the guardian.

Three Magi or Wise Men from the East. *Magi*, a Greek word translated as "wise men" in the King James Version of the Bible, referred to a caste in Arabia, Mesopotamia, and possibly Persia. The men were knowledgeable in many fields and usually were astrologers who combined knowledge of the stars with other knowledge. *Wise men* is a good translation, for they represent just what the name implies—wisdom. Because the traditional story specifies "three" as the number, the Magi symbolize a synthesis of wisdom. The Gospel According to Matthew does not say how many wise men came from the East, but it does mention three gifts, adding myrrh to the gold and frankincense that Isaiah had specified in a passage thought to apply to the birth of the Messiah (Isaiah 60:6). Because the wise men come from the East, the spiritual realm, they symbolize a synthesis or accumulation of all spiritual wisdom. Fillmore calls what they symbolize "the stored-up resources of the soul."[1] Significantly, only the Magi see the star, because only inner wisdom can form a conviction of the inner Christ.

The gifts the Magi bring and their association with astrology indicate that the group of three represents the highest instance or a synthesis of the aspects of the archetype of the magician. The magician is the potentiality for balancing and living in harmony with the spiritual and the material, the supernatural and the natural. The magician archetype is our potentiality for extracting the good from every challenge in the external world and thereby enhancing internal evolution.

Herod. Obviously, Herod represents the negative aspect of the archetype of the king. The metaphysical meaning of Herod has been given. However, it is appropriate to add that one meaning of the name is "heroic." Herod, we have seen, symbolizes the egocentric ego. The meaning of his name implies that the egocentric ego will make heroic efforts to protect itself.

Scribes. Historically, scribes were educated individuals who were often hired to read and write for people who could not. The scribes Herod consulted symbolize thoughts that come to us only from other persons or from books.

Simeon. Simeon was the righteous and devout man in the temple in Jerusalem when Mary and Joseph dedicated Jesus. Among the meanings of the name are "harkening," "obeying," and "understanding." As a man, he represents the thinking nature. His name suggests that he is open to intuition, and he recognizes that the child is the awaited Messiah. Though

Luke does not say he is old, in presentations of the traditional story he usually is, probably because he indicates that having seen the child, he is quite willing to die. Thus, Simeon represents the matured thinking nature that has integrated intuition and accepts the emerging Christ as the purpose for living. He symbolizes the archetype of the wise old man.

Anna. The name *Anna* means "grace." She was the old prophetess who practically lived in the temple. She offered thanks to God for having seen the child and told others about him. Though she appears only briefly, Luke gives her exact age, lineage, and something of her history, indicating that what she symbolizes is very important. She is 84. Her father was Phanuel, a name that means "within the presence of God." Her tribe was Asher, which means "blessedness." She was married for seven years and then widowed, facts that indicated she completed the human feminine role. So she represents the completely realized feeling nature.

Anna is called a prophetess. A prophet receives direct revelations from God, relays them to others, and foretells the future. Thus, Anna represents the positive aspect of the archetype of the crone or wise old woman who is the epitome of spiritual wisdom. Her presence symbolizes the soul's destiny to evolve to the highest state through the grace of God's presence within it.

Every character represents something within us, realized or potential, active in our consciousness or latent in our unconscious. They all play their parts in our personal transformative trips to our spiritual Bethlehem, and they express through each of us in ways unique to the individual. So no two trips will be exactly the same. The trip, remember, symbolizes the process of rebirth through which the higher Self emerges to become the center of consciousness and the integrating force within it. Because your consciousness differs from mine, our rebirth experiences will differ.

Our expressions of the higher Self will also differ. The higher Self is the divine idea of the image of God. God is the infinitely creative mind that antedates any of its ideas and has infinite potential for expression.

And so this great myth is subject to differing interpretations and serves us best when we find the unique meaning for each of us. The explanations and brief interpretations presented in the next chapter provide a framework within which we may discover our own meanings, the ones that guide us on our personal spiritual journeys of transformation.

7

Stages of the Trip

Paul said, "the mystery hidden for ages and generations" is "Christ in you, the hope of glory" (Colossians 1:26-27). The realization of that hope begins when we accept the invitation to take the mystical trip within our consciousness to the stable/cave of Bethlehem. We discover more and more of the glory as we move through each stage of the transformative trip, for at each stage, the power of God is available to assist us.

The mystical journey itself features 12 stages. During each stage, the power of God enhances one of 12 divine or spiritual attributes that constitute the image of God in us. They are the faculties of mind inherited from our Divine Parent. They give us the abilities to deal with the material world, which we use in various ways all our lives. When we turn our minds toward spiritual work, they become active in new, spiritual ways to facilitate our progress.

Twelve stands for cosmic order. Cosmic order results when cycles of spiritual and material activity are in harmony. Transformation is the process by which cosmic order is realized within us. Twelve also stands for salvation. The goal of transformation is salvation from the error of considering ourselves less than we are, of settling for being "only human" when we are, in Truth, human and divine.

At each stage of the mystical trip to Bethlehem, the metaphysical meanings of the characters and elements of the Christmas story bring to consciousness patterns for possible forms of functioning. We cooperate with the transformation process by recognizing which forms we need to incorporate and then by accepting them into our consciousness.

A few patterns may already be active within us, because even to attempt the trip indicates that we have, perhaps unknowingly, completed some stage of the journey. So, although the story presents the 12 stages of transformation in a specific order, to experience transformation we do not need to adhere to that order. Each of us is unique. Many people perform the spiritual tasks in particular stages, not for conscious spiritual growth but for the resolution of their human problems. For instance, people who successfully participate either in 12-step programs to gain freedom from life-spoiling addictions (whether to alcohol, drugs, food, sex, work, or relationships) or in psychotherapy move through many of the stages. Each of us must enter the transformation process at the stage appropriate for his or her present state of consciousness.

The following presentation of the stages includes only brief interpretations of the episodes:

Stage One: Herod the Great

The story is set during the closing years of the reign of Herod the Great.

In Chapter 3, the symbolism of Herod the Great is presented fully. Briefly, he represents the egocentric ego. The fact that Herod is not an admirable character indicates that transformation is a process open to everyone. We cannot earn it. The invitation to participate is an instance of God's grace.

Accepting that invitation calls for exercising our mental faculty of renunciation. Renunciation gives us the ability to change the way we think by giving up inappropriate habitual beliefs and attitudes. Renunciation helps us cleanse our consciousness of erroneous beliefs about ourselves so that we may replace them with Truth. This stage is essential in 12-step programs and productive psychotherapy.

Paradoxically, although the egocentric ego is the only enemy of the Christ, it is when the egocentric ego rules the psyche that we are ready to let the Christ emerge, for then we have an established sense of ourselves as individuals, and the Christ expresses only through individuals. But when the Christ emerges, the *exclusive* reign of the egocentric ego ends.

We need to know ourselves as individuals, for then we can recognize and renounce egocentric tendencies, beliefs, attitudes, and feelings that block expression of the Christ without losing our sense of self. We can then not only see how our own talents and attributes can be used to give expression to the Christ, but we can also resist the temptation to relapse into egocentricity.

Stage Two: The East, the Star, and the Wise Men

This stage takes place before the narrative begins. We know that because when the Magi fail to report back to Herod, he orders the massacre of male infants 2 years old or younger. That indicates that the three wise men first see the star in the East a little before the time when Gabriel appears to Zechariah. In other words, it happens before the first episode.

Metaphysically, it is highly significant that the star appears in the East before the story begins. The East represents the spiritual realm, which is the source of the ultimate Truth about us, symbolized by the star. The Truth is that we are created to express the image of God as the creative principle, the Christ. Only through the mental faculty of wisdom, symbolized by the three wise men, can we grasp the significance of the spiritual nature.

Wisdom is our ability to recognize Truth, even when it is new and strange. It often comes as an intuitive flash and, when we hold it in mind, it guides us toward our true destiny—the expression of the Christ.

The Christ is the rightful ruler of the religious nature (as King of the Jews) for our religious nature reveals the underlying oneness of God with all creation, including ourselves. This is the Truth that is often hidden by conventional religious beliefs and traditional rites. Until we are convinced that we are the direct offspring of God, we are not likely to participate in the process that moves us beyond conventional, traditional religious forms to conscious acceptance of the spiritual nature as the center of the psyche. But once our inner wise men have seen the star and grasped its meaning, we feel compelled to do our part.

Stage Three: Gabriel, Zechariah, John, and Elizabeth

The angel Gabriel appears at the right side of the altar of the temple in Jerusalem where Zechariah, the priest, is burning incense. Gabriel announces that Elizabeth will conceive and bear a son to be named John. John will prepare the way for the Christ. Because Zechariah doubts the incredible news, he loses the power of speech.

The opening event occurs in the temple (symbol of the body) and at the altar (symbol of the meeting place in consciousness between us and God) while incense is burning (symbol of prayer and the presence of Spirit). Thus, we know the story is about a process that can start within a human being during prayer. We know, too, that the process is initiated by God because the angel Gabriel (symbol of a message from God) appears at the right side (symbol of the activity of God) of the altar. The name, Zechariah, meaning "the Lord is remembered," signifies that, for the moment, conventional religious understanding (the Priest) has given way to spiritual consciousness. The mind is open to receive the message, which starts the transformation process, and the mental faculty of understanding is activated in a new way.

The faculty of understanding enables us to recognize and apply the principles that underlie the Truth we have grasped through wisdom. This is the meaning of Gabriel's message: It is never too late to change. The thinking nature (Zechariah) and feeling nature (Elizabeth) can blend to produce a moral nature springing from grace or love and mercy (John) rather than solely from conventional religious forms of right conduct (the Priest). The new moral nature will prepare the consciousness for the rulership of God through the inner Christ.

The mental faculty of understanding must become active in a new way to achieve the goal of transformation; thus, Zechariah loses the power of speech while the foundation for the new understanding is made firm by the feeling nature. Zechariah's loss of speech has two other meanings: It also symbolizes the initial inability to accept the full significance of the message, and it symbolizes the power of God to prevent conventional religious beliefs and practices from interfering with the spiritual process, which forms the new moral nature.

The formerly barren Elizabeth conceives and, with a grateful heart, goes into seclusion for five months.

Elizabeth (God's oath) represents the feeling nature through which God fulfills the promise. Fillmore says she represents the "soul in the feminine or love consciousness."

Since love is the principle of oneness and harmony, Elizabeth represents the feeling of spiritual oneness with other persons, which produces a moral nature based on grace, love, and mercy.

Five is the numerical symbol for the live human being, and the fifth month is usually the time when the fetus becomes active in the uterus. So five months in seclusion suggests the need to meditate upon oneness with other persons until love and mercy become viable ideas in human consciousness. We then understand how to relate spiritually to one another.

Stage Four: Nazareth of Galilee, Mary, and Gabriel

When Elizabeth is six months pregnant, Gabriel appears to her kinswoman, Mary, a virgin who lives in Nazareth in Galilee and is betrothed to Joseph, a descendant of David. Gabriel tells Mary that she will conceive a son to be named Jesus who will be given the throne of David and rule over the "house of Jacob" forever. Mary protests that she is not married. Gabriel explains that the Holy Spirit will cause the miracle. Then he tells her about Elizabeth, adding "with God nothing will be impossible." Mary accepts her task and Gabriel disappears.

The kinship of Mary and Elizabeth indicates the interrelationship of the factors of the soul that each represents.

That this stage is reached in the sixth month of Elizabeth's pregnancy is important. Six symbolizes perfection and harmony, so the sixth month indicates that basic ideas for true morality have become perfectly harmonized with other parts of consciousness. Six also symbolizes the pure or purified soul. Gabriel's appearance in the sixth month indicates that soul is now purified and ready to develop Christ consciousness. Mary, we have seen, represents the purified soul.

This stage of the trip requires that the mental faculty of imagination become involved. Imagination gives us the ability to mentally see or visualize what exists only in potential, what has not yet been expressed. The mind must be able to conceive the idea of the Christ before it can become viable within us.

The purified soul is a potential that can be realized by anyone who can grasp the idea of or imagine the omnipresence of Spirit (Israel). That is symbolized by Mary's living in Nazareth (a village of ordinary people) and considering herself an Israelite (the idea of the omnipresence of God). The idea has a momentum of its own (the literal meaning of Galilee) that stimulates spiritual evolution.

Mary's betrothal to Joseph, a descendant of David (symbol of divine love in human consciousness), foreshadows the integration of divine love with all other attributes of the soul.

Gabriel's message clearly indicates that the higher Self, the Christ, is spiritual. Mary's virginity signifies that the inner Christ emerges not from human activity but solely from the activity of God. Our part is to permit its development and let it take its rightful place as ruler of the psyche.

The ordained name for the child, Jesus (salvation, helper, prosperer), signifies that the idea of the image of God in us has the power to transform every aspect of our lives.

The news about Elizabeth with the reminder that God can do anything foreshadows the fortification of faith, which occurs at the next stage.

Mary's acceptance of her task symbolizes the soul's willingness to fulfill its destiny, to allow the process to occur.

Stage Five: Mary, Elizabeth, and the Birth of John

Mary travels to Zechariah's house in the hill town of Judah to visit Elizabeth. When the women meet, Elizabeth's unborn child stirs and Elizabeth realizes that Mary is to bear the holy child. Both women express praise and thanksgiving.

The hill town of Judah (praise) represents the high state of consciousness in which the faculty of faith adds its power to the activity of the other faculties. That Mary travels to the hill town and enters Zechariah's house (the consciousness of the Priest) indicates that the soul does not abandon the outer forms of religion, but, with the mental faculty of faith now active, fulfills them with a fresh realization of what the forms represent.

The meeting of Mary and Elizabeth signifies that the whole feminine nature is involved. Mary's prayer expresses the power of faith to enrich life.

After three months, Mary returns to Nazareth. Soon Elizabeth's baby is born. Eight days later, he is circumcised. When Zechariah writes on the tablet that the child is to be named John, Zechariah regains his power of speech and uses it first to praise God.

Three is the numerical symbol of synthesis. The soul continues to praise God and fulfill conventional religious forms while synthesis occurs.

After Mary returns to Nazareth (a more ordinary state of consciousness), John (the moral nature and illumined intellect) is born. That signifies that what John represents must appear in ordinary human life.

The eighth day after birth indicates the beginning of a new condition or cycle that features regeneration, rebirth, and eternity. The rite of circumcision is seen by students of symbology and Fillmore as the process of renouncing lower desires. However, since the rite marked the Jews as a people set apart to serve God (Genesis 17:10-13), it is also proper to consider that circumcision symbolizes dedication of the religious nature to the service of true spirituality.

When Zechariah obeys God and names the child John, he regains the power of speech and immediately praises God. This indicates that the new understanding (enhanced by faith) has imbued religious thoughts with a spiritual dimension. The idea of grace has been accepted in consciousness, and the thinking nature is ready to hear the next angelic message.

Stage Six: Joseph and Gabriel

In Nazareth, Joseph realizes that Mary is pregnant. His first impulse is to divorce her, but Gabriel appears in a dream and tells him Mary is carrying the destined savior. So Joseph marries her, but does not consummate the marriage until after the baby is born.

When awake, Joseph reacts in a conventional way to Mary's pregnancy. That represents how most of us first react to the idea that we are designed to express the image of God. It disturbs us, because to accept and act upon the idea calls for a complete revision of consciousness, so we want to get rid of it. That is how the faculty of will operates on the human level. The will gives us the ability to choose what we shall do. We have freedom of choice because we are made in God's image, and our will is like God's will, absolutely free. God does not compel us to feel, think, or do anything, not even what leads to our highest good. The will is also the executive faculty. Once we have made the choice, the will marshals all our faculties to help us act upon the decision.

Joseph receives the message in his sleep when conscious thought is quiet and the message from Spirit can come through. In addition, the power of the egocentric ego has already been weakened by the use of the faculty of renunciation in the first stage, and the faculties of wisdom, understanding, imagination, and faith have been stimulated in succeeding stages.

61

Moreover, the name Joseph means "he shall increase progressively." That indicates the thinking nature can expand to accept the idea. The faculty of will can operate in harmony with God's purpose.

Joseph's obedience to Gabriel's message signifies the activity of will on the spiritual level. It readies the thinking nature to do its part in the process of transformation.

Stage Seven: The Census, Bethlehem, the Inn, Cave, Ass, Ox, Swaddling Cloths, and Manger

A world census is being made, which requires people to be counted in their tribal cities. Being close to term, Mary rides an ass to make the trip with Joseph to Bethlehem, the city of David. The inn is filled, so the innkeeper has them and the ass stay in the stable-cave where he keeps his ox. They are barely settled when Jesus is born. Mary wraps him in swaddling cloths and lays him in the manger.

Mary and Joseph travel to Bethlehem because they must fulfill a worldly duty. Thus, the child is born in Bethlehem. That indicates that the transformation process continues even while we are doing whatever life requires of us. The mental faculty of strength is active to enable us to persist in our spiritual purpose despite material inconvenience or distraction. Strength also gives us patience, endurance, and spiritual stamina. It holds us firmly on course so that we may achieve our goal. All thoughts and feelings acquired from experience with the material environment are called together (world census) when the soul of a living person (Mary on the ass) is about to let the higher Self emerge. The emergence must occur in a consciousness of omnipresent spiritual substance (Bethlehem). The feeling and thinking nature as well as love and wisdom (all symbolized by Mary and Joseph) are in harmony (married) and need to be isolated from everyday consciousness with its mixture of thoughts and feelings (the crowded inn). They must retreat into the collective unconscious (stable-cave) for the emergence of the idea of a new spiritual identity (birth of the Christ child).

The emergence of our higher Self increases strength, for it reconciles the opposites in consciousness (ox and ass) and directs the energy of the shadow (ass) toward spiritually creative purposes.

Since the newly emerged higher Self is the divine idea of God's image, it has infinite potentialities. However, it has been born to a specific soul (Mary) and must accept the restraints or apparent limitations of individualized expression. The restraints, symbolized by the swaddling cloths, also focus the strength of the emergent higher Self where it needs to be focused on being the stable governing center of consciousness for the particular individual. While it begins its work, it is surrounded by all it needs to nurture it (lying in a manger).

Stage Eight: Night, Light, the Shepherds, Flock, and Lamb

That night, in the midst of a great light, Gabriel appears to shepherds watching their flock in a nearby field. Gabriel calms their fear by announcing the birth of the Christ, a gift from God to them and all people. He tells them where to find the child and a heavenly choir joins him. The shepherds hurry to Bethlehem and enter the cave. After telling Mary and Joseph what the angel said and giving their gift of a lamb, they return to the field rejoicing. Mary is very quiet.

Night is another symbol for the unconscious. The *great light* or what Luke calls "the glory of the Lord" symbolizes Spirit, which is always present in the collective unconscious. Shepherds, of course, being common people, symbolize something present in everyone. Specifically, they represent forces that guard the seven human virtues, attributes symbolized by the flock of sheep: honesty, prudence, temperance, courage, justice, charity, and compassion.

Those virtues and guardians are all expressions of love as the principle of oneness, which produces harmony within us and in our relationships. The gift of the Christ is for the shepherds and everyone else, so the gift is evidence of divine love. And so the mental faculty of love has become active as a spiritual attribute.

The guardian forces are sensitive to the presence of Spirit and ready to receive and respond to Gabriel's announcement. Their immediate trip to Bethlehem indicates readiness to serve the higher Self. The gift of the lamb symbolizes recognition that the potential for purity, innocence, sweetness, harmlessness, and forgiveness (all instances of love) belong to the Christ. Mary's silence suggests the need to remain still and allow the Christ to continue to unfold.

Stage Nine: Naming, House, Jerusalem, Temple, Simeon, and Anna

On the eighth day, the day of circumcision, Joseph names the child Jesus. He moves the family to a house in Bethlehem. After waiting the required two months, they go to the temple in Jerusalem to perform the required purification rites, to sacrifice a pair of turtledoves or two young pigeons, and to dedicate Jesus. Simeon, an old man, follows them from the temple door and, inspired by the Holy Spirit, he takes the child in his arms and blesses him. Anna, the 84-year-old prophetess who was always in the temple, joins Mary, Joseph, and Simeon. She thanks God for the child.

During this stage, the mental faculty of order guides us through the proper sequence of inner events.

Again, the eighth day indicates the beginning of a new cycle, regeneration, and rebirth. A new cycle begins for us when we acknowledge that the Christ is God's offspring and belongs to God (circumcision). We experience regeneration and rebirth when the intellect (Joseph) accepts the new idea of the Christ (the child) as the saving, helping, prospering factor (naming the child Jesus) in consciousness (moving into a house).

The two months' wait stands for a period during which inner equilibrium is established. From the Jungian perspective, two indicates that the idea of the higher Self is being established in consciousness.

The whole body (temple) is at peace (Jerusalem) when the new idea is connected to conventional religious ideas (performance of required rites). Both the thinking and feeling natures achieve maturity as they respond with divine wisdom and recognize the rulership of the Christ (Simeon and Anna).

Stage Ten: The Wise Men from the East, Jerusalem, Herod, the Gifts

The family returns to the house in Bethlehem. Soon three Magi from the East ride camels into Jerusalem. Believing the star is leading them to the newborn King of the Jews, they go to the seat of government to ask where he is. Herod feels threatened when he hears about the wise men's quest. He asks the priests and scribes where the expected king was to be born and they say in Bethlehem. Herod summons the wise men, finds out when they first saw the star, and sends them to Bethlehem, telling them to return to tell him where to find the child so that he may pay his respects.

The star leads the Magi to the house of Joseph. They enter, bow to worship the child, and give their gifts of gold, frankincense, and myrrh. That night, they are warned in a dream not to go back to Herod. They go home by another route.

At this stage, the mental faculty of power enhances all the other faculties with an infusion of spiritual energy that protects us from error.

Accumulated spiritual wisdom perseveres (the Magi from the East riding camels) in the search for the Christ, pausing first in peace of mind (Jerusalem) where we might expect the higher Self to emerge. Although peace of mind (Jerusalem) is a high state of consciousness, it is not as high as the consciousness of omnipresent substance (Bethlehem). The egocentric ego (Herod) can achieve and abide in peace of mind, but it fears the Christ. The search threatens the egocentric ego. It seems to cooperate, but it only wants to protect itself. Spiritual wisdom continues the search (follows the star).

Spiritual wisdom recognizes and enters the consciousness in which the masculine and feminine natures have achieved perfect harmony and are serving the higher Self (Mary, Joseph, and the child in Joseph's house in Bethlehem). Spiritual wisdom recognizes that enduring value (gold), transformative power (frankincense), and eternal attraction (myrrh) are powerful attributes of the Christ and that the Christ is the rightful ruler of the psyche.

Spiritual wisdom also is alert to potential danger from the egocentric ego (warning in a dream) and immediately bypasses peace of mind to return to the East (spiritual dimension of consciousness).

Stage Eleven: The Flight to Egypt and Massacre of the Innocents

The same night the wise men receive their warning, Gabriel appears to Joseph in a dream to tell him to take the mother and child to Egypt because Herod plans to kill the child. Immediately, Joseph arises, puts Mary and Jesus on the ass, and the family starts for Egypt. The enraged Herod, not knowing exactly where to find the child, orders the massacre of all male children 2 years old and younger in and around Bethlehem.

The function of the mental faculty of zeal to inspire us with devotion to the higher Self is symbolized in this stage of the trip.

Intuitively, the intellectual nature realizes that the Christ must be protected from the destructive activity of the egocentric ego (Gabriel's command to take the mother and child to Egypt and Joseph's obedience). In the attempt to obliterate all thought of a higher Self, the egocentric ego destroys every new thought about spiritual substance (the children in and around Bethlehem). But the true higher Self has been safely hidden (gone to Egypt).

Stage Twelve: Death of Herod and the Return to Nazareth

A year or so after the massacre, Herod dies. In Egypt, Gabriel appears again to Joseph to tell him that it is safe for the family to return to Israel. However, when Joseph realizes that Herod's son now rules in Jerusalem, he does not go back to Bethlehem but takes them to Nazareth.

That the higher Self has survived is evidence of the activity of the mental faculty of life.

When the egocentric ego is no longer the center of consciousness (death of Herod), the Christ can safely activate spiritual thoughts (Gabriel's message to return to Israel). But since peace of mind (Jerusalem in Judea) is the state of consciousness in which the egocentric ego (Herod's son) can again become powerful, the intellect (Joseph) protects the developing Christ by surrounding it with simple or unsophisticated spiritual thoughts of an apparently ordinary consciousness (Israelite inhabitants of Nazareth).

To make your own transformative journey, begin at whichever stage you believe is your starting point. No matter where you begin, go at the pace Spirit sets. Usually, it will not be rapid, because there will be habits of thought and action that need to be changed, and such changes require time. Allow for periods of rest between stages of the journey, for during each resting period, new habits of thought and action are formed and become fixed in consciousness.

The chapters that follow give suggestions to help you to make your own trip to Bethlehem.

The Inner
Journey

$$\boxed{8}$$

Stage One
Renunciation:
Weakening Egocentricity

Preparation for the Trip

Long before the departure date, wise travelers make careful preparation. Gathering information is a part of preparation, and that is what we have been doing so far. Learning the metaphysical meanings of the elements and stages in the traditional Christmas story is not the trip; it is preparation for the trip. The trip itself is a mystical experience. It is an inner process that gradually leads us in consciousness first to an invisible point beyond space and time, where we become aware that the abiding presence of God is the all-providing substance, life, and intelligence that nurtures us and our emerging higher Self, and then back to our world ready to express our whole nature in daily life.

The renunciation of egocentricity is the first stage of the trip—the final preparation. During the information gathering, we learned that the Christ is born when Herod is king and that Herod symbolizes a well-established egocentric ego. So, although each person begins the trip to Bethlehem at the stage of consciousness they have already reached, to participate in the process of transformation without losing the sense of identity as human beings we all need a well-established ego. Furthermore, until we complete the entire process and the Christ rules the psyche, in all likelihood any well-established ego will be to some degree egocentric.

That is because egocentricity develops in response to the environment in which we must perform the basic human task—to survive.

In the Christmas story, Herod is the only enemy of the newborn Christ. It is wise, then, before we start the mystical trip to divest the inner Herod of as much power and influence as we can. That involves becoming aware of our own egocentric traits and disposing of those that could block the way to Bethlehem.

Moreover, awareness of our own egocentricity protects us from making the dangerous error of identifying our sense of self with any archetype that arises from the collective unconscious, such as the archetype of the mother. That error leads to *ego inflation*. Very simply put, in a state of ego inflation, a person mistakes the part for the whole and lets the archetype define the self or determine behavior or both. If a woman identifies with the mother archetype, she will not develop as a many-sided person and will probably be overprotective and demanding. Ego inflation delays or prevents transformation because it puts one under the influence of an archetype rather than helping the individual to integrate its potential into consciousness. In a state of ego inflation, the egocentric traits compatible with the archetype become exaggerated rather than weakened.

Egocentric traits are habitual coping mechanisms that have helped us survive. Because they are habits, even while we participate in the transformation process, they tend to exert influence. Our sense of identity is deeply entrenched. Habits of thought—about who and what we are, and what we can be and do—change slowly. Thus, every type of egocentric ego has a Herod-like tendency to defend its sovereignty. No matter at which stage we begin the trip, we need to be able to recognize our own egocentric traits, for only then can we overcome them whenever they reassert themselves.

Egocentricity Defined

Beginning in infancy, even before we can speak, we try different ways to let our parents or other caretakers know our needs for food, sleep, comfort, and attention. We repeat the ways that result in satisfaction, and they become habits. As we grow through the phases of early development, we also acquire desires for pleasurable conditions and things not related to survival. Again we try different ways to get what we want and adopt those that work. The ways we learn vary with the kind of environment in which we learn them. The people around us reinforce our learning with their responses to us. Little by little, we develop a sense of identity as we equate what we believe we are with what we believe we must do to survive and to have what we want. Because our first responsibility is to survive, we protect our sense of identity in some fashion and our egos are to some degree egocentric.

In the early discussion of the significance of Herod in the Christmas story, the four basic egocentric ego types identified by the Jungian analyst, Fritz Kunkel, were briefly mentioned. They are discussed more thoroughly below. While reading the more detailed listing of beliefs that distinguish the egocentric types, remember these important points: No type is gender-related and no normal, sane person is a pure example of any one egocentric type. Each type is an archetype. It is a possible pattern for responding to one's environment.

Kunkel's Four Egocentric Types[1]

The Clinging Vine. Clinging vine egocentricity tends to develop in girls and boys with lower vitality than their relatively indulgent, overprotective, and overly helpful parents and caretakers. Oddly, clinging vines believe they please people by continuing to be helpless.

Adults with clinging vine egos remain childishly dependent. They believe they need some reliable, mighty person or institution to tell them what to do or to take care of them. Feeling powerless, they can imagine nothing worse than to be abandoned or forced to depend on themselves, so they believe they must be guaranteed security and protection. To them, the world at large seems frightening and unfriendly.

Adult clinging vines have little tolerance for suffering and play upon the sympathy of family, even their own children, and associates to relieve it. They use the same kind of weakness, helplessness, illness, and ignorance that got them what they needed or wanted as children to persuade others to do for them what they believe they cannot do for themselves. They gain attention by being miserable and talking about their suffering and problems. They usually do not want advice about how they can solve their problems; they believe that someone else must solve them for them. In extreme cases, clinging vines become public charges.

The Star. Star egocentricity tends to develop in girls and boys with higher vitality than their relatively indulgent, protective, and admiring parents and caretakers. They use coaxing, cleverness, and charm more than tears, whining, or helplessness to get what they need or want.

Adults with star egos believe that getting others to notice, admire, and like them can not only get others to take care of mundane or difficult situations but also pleases others. Sometimes stars work hard to be the best at what they do, but more often they settle for appearing the best and do not necessarily achieve much in the world.

Convinced of their own cleverness and charm, they cannot tolerate indifference, ridicule, dislike, and rivalry and tend to counter such responses to them with *prima donna* behavior. The worst things that can happen to a star are to be ignored and to lose dignity or admiration.

The Nero or Tyrant. Nero or tyrant egocentricity tends to develop in boys or girls with high vitality reared by harsh, demanding, strict, or indifferent parents and caretakers. Feeling that the people around them are against them or uncaring, they believe they must wheedle, pester, threaten, or behave violently to get what they need or want.

Because any type of egocentricity can become tyrannical, the name of one of the most tyrannical Roman rulers, Nero, is given to this type. Nero was a persecutor of Christians.

Adults with tyrant egocentricity believe that power over other people is essential. They have no interest in pleasing people. Instead, they demand obedience rather than cooperation. Believing that the world is hostile, they have little or no concern for the welfare of other people.

The worst things that can happen to them are to lose their control over people, be disobeyed, and be put in a subordinate position.

The Turtle. Turtle egocentricity tends to develop in boys or girls with lower vitality than their harsh, demanding, strict, or indifferent parents and caretakers. They feel overwhelmed by the apparent harshness of life, become hopeless, accept whatever satisfaction for needs they happen to receive, and give up asking for what they want or attempting to please anyone.

Adults with turtle egocentricity remain as apparently stoical as they were as children. They attempt to control their world by ignoring it. They believe themselves incapable of dealing with people and ask for nothing more than to be left alone and not disturbed in any way. They dislike being touched and cannot tolerate being stirred up emotionally.

Obviously, a pure example of any egocentric type would be a caricature. Self-examination usually reveals that we have some traits of two or more of the types. It is not unusual for a man to behave like a "Nero" at work and a "turtle" at home or for a woman to behave like a "star" at committee meetings and a "clinging vine" with her husband. In addition, we are likely to have some egocentric traits and beliefs that vary from those of Kunkel's four types but that also develop as we struggle to survive in our family of origin. These also contribute to our sense of self.

The Functional Home

Studies of adults who grew up in dysfunctional homes show that they tend to continue to enact the survival or coping roles assumed in childhood. Since it is the rare childhood home that was not dysfunctional, at least from a child's perspective, at some point most people recognize that at some time they have filled one or more of the coping roles. Some coping characteristics and beliefs may even have persisted as part of their sense of identity.

Before we examine the coping roles, we need to know the general characteristics of both functional and dysfunctional homes.

In a functional home, the parents or other adult caretakers give children unconditional love by word and act. Though boundaries are set to assure privacy and safety for all family members, rules of behavior are reasonable and enforced with love, not punishment. Adults are sensitive to the needs of the children and honor their differences. While they encourage achievement, they make allowance for apparent failure, because their expectations are realistic. Adults are reliable; they keep promises or, if they cannot, they explain why plans have changed and generally make up for disappointments. Parents are present for their children, interested in their concerns, and available for comfort and companionship. Children feel free to express their thoughts, feelings, and preferences.

Obviously, the above describes an ideal rather than an actuality.

The Dysfunctional Home

In a dysfunctional home, love for the children is usually conditional or nonexistent. Often a home is dysfunctional because the adults are deeply troubled, perhaps mentally or physically ill, addicted, or otherwise impaired. Personal boundaries are unclear and rules of behavior are either lacking or very rigid. If rules are broken, punishment may be severe. Children's privacy may be invaded. Adults may have favorites, smothering one child with lavish attention while ignoring the needs of another. Expectations, if there are any, are often unrealistic. Achievement may be demanded or ignored. Failure may be punished. Children may be abused or expected to behave more maturely than their age warrants. Promises are broken without explanation. Children are not free to express their thoughts, feelings, and preferences and have difficulty trusting anyone.

Sometimes illness, death, divorce, economic conditions, work demands, war, or other circumstance that children cannot understand makes some aspect of an otherwise functional home dysfunctional during a crucial developmental stage in a child's life. If the situation endures for long, the child adopts characteristics of one or more of the coping roles.

Coping roles are also archetypal.

Coping Roles

Family Hero. Though possessing some characteristics of Kunkel's "star," family heroes seem to achieve more and exhibit more concern for other people than do stars. As children, they are usually a source of pride for the family. They tend to work hard and be visibly successful in school or some other public arena. They are well-behaved and genuinely liked by peers and adults. They please people by being helpful "little adults" who, in severely dysfunctional homes, may also be caretakers who believe they must assume parental responsibilities toward their siblings and even toward the weaker parent. Inwardly, such children usually feel inadequate and ashamed of the family, but they strive to appear strong and to protect the family image.

Adults who were family heroes tend to be "workaholics," obsessed with doing their duty, being "right," and maintaining a good public image. If they have been caretakers, they are likely to attract and marry or be intimately associated with much weaker or troubled persons. Feeling responsible for everyone else in their families, they readily sacrifice their own needs and desires to get adult siblings out of trouble. Some caretakers remain single and continue to care for a parent or other family member.

Not surprisingly, family heroes, particularly the caretakers, gravitate into the helping professions.

Scapegoat. Scapegoats develop in severely dysfunctional homes. Such children are often blamed for the family problems and hide their feelings of hurt, guilt, and rejection by withdrawing into sullen silence like the "turtle" or by openly displaying hostility, defiance, and anger. As a rule, since they feel inadequate and will not compete with the family hero, they do poorly in school, where they either withdraw or, like the "star," demand attention but with disruptive behavior. These children tend to substitute their peers for their family. They often join gangs and do what pleases the gang leaders.

As adults, scapegoats are likely to have difficulty holding jobs and may get in trouble with the law. Many scapegoats become criminals or die violently.

The scapegoats who receive and accept help become good citizens and often do work that calls for courage and compassion. Since they understand rebels, they make sensitive counselors for troubled young people.

Lost Child. Lost children are a combination of fragile "clinging vines" and sensitive "turtles" who do not develop thick shells but become instead almost invisible. Whether their home was severely dysfunctional or dysfunctional for only a crucial developmental period, lost children fear attention. They withdraw from conflict. They also have difficulty making friends. Rarely seen and seldom heard, lost children make few or no demands and thus provide a kind of relief for troubled adults who seem pleased not to have to worry about them. Because they spend so much time alone, normally intelligent lost children often have rich imaginations and, though they are considered to be dreamers, they frequently do well in school. However, having little vitality, lost children may be sickly, but even then, they tend to suffer in silence and, as a consequence, many develop handicaps or die young.

As adults, lost children believe that loneliness is their lot and make little or no effort to initiate close relationships. They feel unimportant and have difficulty making decisions. In short, though some lost children become quietly creative adults, they generally have so little sense of their own identity that they seldom assert themselves.

With proper help, lost children can become independent, self-reliant, and unassuming but assertive adults.

Mascot. Mascots are a combination of the clinging vine and the star. Though fragile, immature, and fearful, they crave attention and tend to please people by being funny. They also tend to be hyperactive, to have a short attention span, and to have a learning disability. If compulsive clowns, they relieve their own tension and family tension with humor.

As adults, they tend to find hero-type mates who will take care of them, and in social situations they are the "life of the party." If not helped to overcome their immaturity, they are subject to stress-related ailments and, to relieve their own tension, may become substance abusers.

With proper help, they, too, can become self-reliant, retain their sense of humor, but drop the role of clown and simply make life more pleasant by helping other people play.

With the foregoing information, we can identify the mixture of specific egocentric traits that can hinder conscious acceptance of our own spiritual nature and the sovereignty of the Christ. Fortunately, there are proven techniques that weaken egocentricity and help us overcome it. It is wise to learn and use them because they help us resist acting upon any egocentric trait that reappears.

Perhaps no one is ever completely immune to the temptation to behave in egocentric ways. But we can resist the temptation, as incidents in the life of Jesus illustrate. After John the Baptist baptized him, Jesus withdrew to the wilderness to fast and pray. It was then that temptation to egocentricity arose. The "devil" who came to tempt him symbolizes the egocentric ego. First, it tempted Jesus to use the power of the Christ to become completely self-sufficient like the "turtle" by turning stones into bread. Then it tempted him to become a "star" by performing a spectacular public feat. Finally, it tempted him to become a "Nero" by conquering the world. Jesus refused each temptation with a statement of Truth and finally said, "Begone, Satan! for it is written, 'You shall worship the Lord your God and him only shall you serve'" (Matthew 4:1-11).

Symbolically, the egocentric ego arose again in the guise of Peter, not long after Peter recognized Jesus as the Christ. Jesus then plainly told the disciples about the danger He faced, and Peter "rebuked" Him. What form the rebuke took, Mark does not say, but Peter must have told Jesus to use the Christ power to protect Himself, for Jesus said, "Get behind me, Satan! For you are not on the side of God, but of men" (Mark 8:27-33).

Any temptation to use the Christ power to avoid one's spiritual task or solely for one's material benefit comes from the egocentric ego. Indeed, we are safe in saying that the egocentric ego is the "devil." Because our own sense of identity is a product of our own thinking, we can use the same method Jesus used to change our thinking and so divest the egocentric ego of power. We can remember the Truth by using certain well-tried, effective techniques to overcome specific egocentric traits. In fact, the techniques are effective even if we do not identify specific traits.

The techniques that follow may be used before beginning the mystical trip to Bethlehem and anytime during or after it when egocentricity challenges the right of the Christ to rule our consciousness or attempts to destroy it.

To Weaken Herod: Use Denials and Affirmations

This is a method used to change the way we habitually think and feel and, therefore, behave. *Denials* are statements that declare unwanted, outgrown, or negative thoughts, feelings, beliefs, and attitudes about ourselves, other persons, and circumstances or conditions are powerless to determine our behavior. Denials weaken Herod by convincing us that we are no longer children at the mercy of the outer world but adults who can take charge of our own lives and behave differently because we can think differently about ourselves. Immediately after using a denial, we can start thinking differently by using an affirmation to replace the undesirable thought, feeling, belief, or attitude with a desirable one.

Affirmations are positive statements that declare the Truth about ourselves, other people, situations, and circumstances. With affirmations, we acknowledge the presence and power of God active within us and everyone and everything. Denials and affirmations are particularly effective when we recognize that we have identified with ways of thinking, feeling, and acting that are typical of specific egocentric types or coping roles or a combination of them. A generalized denial such as either of the following could be helpful:

1. *The thoughts, feelings, beliefs, and attitudes of the (clinging vine, star, Nero, turtle, family hero, scapegoat, lost child, or mascot) are powerless over my Christ self.*
2. *I reject the rule of (here name the type or role) over my consciousness.*

The following affirmations are appropriate to use after either of those denials:

1. *I am a spiritual being living in a spiritual universe governed by spiritual law.*
2. *God is the only presence and power in me and in my life.*

If we recognize only a few egocentric characteristics or coping role traits, we can deny power to them individually. The following denial may be modified to weaken the power of an unwanted characteristic or trait: *I reject the belief that I must be (dependent, admired, obeyed, left alone, over-responsible, rebellious, lonely, always amusing).*

Effective affirmations to use after that denial are:

1. *I am now free to express (my higher Self, the image of God, the Christ of my Being) with anyone, anywhere.*
2. *God guides me as I express my true nature.*
3. *God helps me be (here state the desired attribute).*

After using denials and affirmations, it is important to follow through with appropriate action. If the prospect of behaving in an unfamiliar way seems frightening, a simple declaration like either of the following can help:

1. *There is nothing to fear, for God is here.*
2. *God is with me.*

Because denials and affirmations change mental habits, it is a good practice to use them the first thing in the morning to set the new habit for the day and just before going to sleep at night, so that thoughts about the new habit become fixed in the subconscious.

To Weaken Herod: Use the Burning Technique

If, despite repeated use of denial and affirmation, some egocentric traits persist, the burning technique can help. A burning is a symbolic process that impresses the subconscious mind with the seriousness of our intention to be rid of thought habits that underlie recurring mental, emotional, physical, or spiritual challenges.

In the process of a burning, we reclaim the power or vital energy from the hidden, false, or no longer appropriate thoughts, feelings, beliefs, and attitudes that underlie the challenges. Since the egocentric ego, which we form entirely with our own thoughts, is the only challenger of the Christ, a burning is an effective means of dealing with it. The process involves spoken and written denials and affirmations that stimulate the subconscious mind to reveal the thoughts that are the origins of our egocentric traits. During it, we may become aware of statements or mottoes by which we have defined ourselves; or, because egocentricity begins in childhood, we may remember long forgotten and perhaps traumatic incidents during which the thoughts became part of our beliefs about ourselves.

Before undertaking a burning, assure yourself of privacy and have writing materials at hand and a safe place to burn paper. Since the process releases the vital energy that had been trapped in thoughts and was required to repress traumatic memories, arrange to complete the burning at least four hours before bedtime.

Instructions for the Burning Technique

1. Silently or aloud, affirm the omnipresence of God. Use any statement you wish and repeat it until you feel a sense of conviction.
2. Silently or aloud, affirm that memories are powerless to disturb or harm you. Repeat until you feel a sense of conviction. This is necessary

to give the subconscious mind permission to release material you may have deliberately suppressed.

3. Silently or aloud, declare: "I now release the thoughts, feelings, beliefs, and attitudes that cause me to live like a _____." In the blank, name the egocentric type or types or coping role or roles you recognize. If you are having difficulty with only a specific trait, you might wish to make this declaration: "I now release the thoughts, feelings, beliefs, and attitudes that cause me to always have to be _____." In the blank specify the trait, for example, *helpless, charming, boss, undisturbed, caretaker, angry, afraid, noticed.*

4. Head the first sheet of paper with these words: "I now release these errors. I loose them, I let them go, and I let God have God's perfect way with them."

5. Sit quietly, and as memories or thoughts come, begin to write but do not look at what you are writing. You do not want to impress what you write on the subconscious mind; you want to release it. Close your eyes or look away. If memories come, do not describe them; simply write the feeling, belief, or attitude associated with each incident. Do not censor. Write whatever comes, even what seems positive; it may simply no longer be appropriate. Use as many sheets of paper as needed but write on one side only and turn each page face down as you finish it.

6. When the flow stops, fold the paper so you cannot read what you have written and tear it into strips while you say or think, "I now release these errors. I loose them, I let them go, and I let God have God's perfect way with them."

7. Burn the paper as you say or think, "Divine love now consumes these errors. The energy is released to be reused in a new and better form." Repeat until all the paper is reduced to ashes.

8. Thank God for your freedom to let the Christ be born in you. If the purpose of your burning was to deny power to some specific trait, you may wish to affirm your power to express its opposite.

9. Dispose of the ashes reverently, perhaps by burying them in a garden or planter. Remember the traits formed of the old thoughts, feelings, beliefs, and attitudes once enabled you to survive.

We may do a burning whenever we feel the need. Suppose, for example, a thought connected with one memory haunts you. Do the first two steps, but for Step 3 declare, "I now release the thoughts, feelings, beliefs, and attitudes that are causing me to remember how afraid I was when my parents shouted at each other," then complete the rest of the steps.

A burning is not a magical practice. It is a spiritual technique that helps us become aware that much human behavior is not inborn but is the result of our own thinking and can be changed to reflect the Truth— that we are designed to be positive and creative. A burning brings to consciousness the no-longer-appropriate and negative thoughts about ourselves so we can replace them with positive and creative thoughts. As our thinking changes, our behavior changes, and people's responses to us change. In this way, we revise our sense of identity and open ourselves to the activity of God within us.

Knowing how to weaken and eventually overcome Herod, we can confidently begin the mystical, transformative trip to Bethlehem.

9

Stage Two
Wisdom: Following the Star

Stage Two of the mystical trip to Bethlehem takes place before any incident in the traditional Christmas story. According to the story's chronology, the Magi must have had their first glimpse of the star months before Mary learned that she would give birth to the Christ. Because Herod ordered the murder of baby boys 2 years old and younger, the star had to have appeared before or about the time of Gabriel's visit to Zechariah with the startling news that he would father a son named John, who would be the forerunner of the Lord.

The Magi, remember, are the only characters in the story to see the star. The shepherds in Luke's account see "a great light," not a star. Because the writer of the Gospel of Matthew in all probability considered the star to be a heavenly being rather than a nonliving object, it is understandable that only the Magi or wise men could see it. As metaphysical figures, the Magi represent the accumulated wisdom of the ages; as psychological figures, they represent the highest aspect of the archetype of the magician. Understood from either approach, they symbolize our innate potential for receiving divine ideas and cooperating with the wisdom and creative activity of God.

When something stirs our inner Magi to action, the mystical trip to Bethlehem begins. Or, like the shepherds, we see a great light, so to speak. The light gradually reveals the truth about us as we move in consciousness from the murky notion of ourselves as mortal, limited creatures isolated from one another and from God, toward the bright view of ourselves as eternal, unlimited spiritual beings inseparably united with one another and with God.

Regardless of where we might think we are on the route to Bethlehem, we benefit by starting this mystical experience at Stage Two with contemplation of the star, for it will stimulate intuition and show us where we really are.

Because mystical experiences take place within our own minds and hearts, they may be expedited through meditation. Meditation is a deeply personal process, and one that can be physically, mentally, emotionally, and spiritually beneficial to those who practice it regularly. There are many ways to meditate, and we are free to select the method most effective for us. An experienced meditator may use a familiar method or the following simple method, which presents any number of choices and is suitable for beginners.

Instructions for Meditation

1. Reserve 20 minutes or more of uninterrupted quiet time. If desired, set a timer or alarm clock. This is a special, sacred time, so silence the phone.
2. Sit or lie comfortably, but with your back straight, arms and legs uncrossed, and eyes closed to shut out distractions.
3. For about 10 breaths or until nothing seems to exist except breath, focus attention on breathing. Do not adjust it; just notice it.
4. For another 10 breaths or until the body is relaxed and peaceful, think of nothing on the inhale and, on the exhale, think of a one-syllable word that invokes a sense of security, such as *God, life, love, peace, joy, Christ,* or a one-syllable word appropriate for the subject of the meditation. For instance, either the word *star* or *light* would be appropriate for meditating on the star. (If, during the inhale, it is difficult to achieve a blank mind, think the word "nothing" or imagine a white screen.)
5. For this step, choose any one or a combination of the following:

a. Let thoughts about the subject of the meditation form spontaneously. If unrelated thoughts arise, gently dismiss them or let them drift away and return for a while to the chosen one-syllable word in Step 4.

b. Direct the flow of thought by using an appropriate favorite quotation or affirmation or one from the list of suggestions that follows the meditation instructions.

c. Direct the flow of thought by adapting the appropriate suggested meditation, listening to a recording of it, or by devising an original meditation. If desired, combine with the following suggestion.

d. Direct the flow of thought by focusing on light of a suggested color or substitute a preferred color. This may be done before or after meditating on each part of the story in a manner like the one suggested later in this chapter.

6. Remain still until the time is finished. Sometimes meditators lose awareness for a while and reach the state of consciousness called "the Silence." Allow it to happen. This is the aim of meditation, for it is during the Silence that divine ideas are communicated directly from Spirit to us.

7. When the time is finished, rest quietly, noticing your breathing for about 10 breaths. Often people drift back into the Silence for a while. If that happens, simply notice your breathing when awareness returns.

8. The return to an ordinary state of consciousness should be gentle. Let your eyelids flutter open and become aware of your body and surroundings gradually. Give thanks to God for the experience and get up slowly.

Quotations for the Star

"... A star shall come forth out of Jacob ..."—Numbers 24:17

"... Praise him, all you shining stars!"—Psalm 148:3

"The people who walked in darkness have seen a great light ..."—Isaiah 9:2

"... We have seen his star in the East ..."—Matthew 2:2

"... The star which they had seen in the East went before them ..."—Matthew 2:9

Quotations for Wisdom

"The Lord gives wisdom."—Proverbs 2:6

"Wisdom will come into your [my] heart."—Proverbs 2:10

"I have counsel and sound wisdom, I have insight ..."
—Proverbs 8:14

"Wisdom is a fountain of life ..."—Proverbs 16:22

"The wisdom from above is first pure, then peaceable, gentle, open to reason, full of mercy and good fruits, without uncertainty or insincerity."—James 3:17

Affirmations for the Star

The star of the East illumines my way to Bethlehem.
I am guided and illumined by the Christmas star.
My inner wise men see and follow the star.
The light of God reveals my potential.

Affirmations for Wisdom

I am open and responsive to the wisdom of God.
I am wise with the wisdom of Spirit.
Spiritual wisdom guides me to express my higher Self.
Spiritual wisdom is mine by divine right.

Meditation on the Star

It is a cloudless night, and the sky is filled with stars. I stand on a high place, a hill, rooftop, or tower, with two robed companions. We are Magi, who decipher messages written by the Lord of Light in the patterns of the stars. This night, we watch as the constellation of the Jews rises on the eastern horizon. Within it is a point of light we have never seen before.

To us, the new star heralds the birth of a new king, One who will rule the world as the agent of the Lord of Light.

I focus upon the rising point of light as its glow brightens. The light radiates and streams into the center of my very being. Its cool brilliance dispels all darkness and I see what I need to see. The light reveals all that I need to know about myself and the way I must travel. In silence, I rest secure, knowing that the light makes all things clear.

The Use of Color for Meditation

Because light has archetypal associations with God as well as both wisdom and understanding, an effective way to begin meditation on any stage of the mystical trip would be to focus for a while on either color suggested for the star, or on yellow or gold—colors associated with wisdom and understanding—or with a color suggested for the stage. Doing so can keep us in touch with the inner Magi. Most adults have unknowingly reached some stage of the trip already, and meditation on the star helps clarify individual tasks. To begin meditation on each stage of the trip with a brief meditation on the star, the following pattern could be used in conjunction with the instructions for meditation. For the star meditation, use either clear white or iridescent light.

Introductory Star Meditation

After the first three steps of the meditation technique, do the following:

1. Breathe normally. For 10 or more breaths, think of nothing or the word *nothing* or visualize a white screen on the inhale, and, on the exhale, think *star* or *light*.
2. Then, for 10 or more breaths, imagine white or iridescent light entering through the crown of the head. On the inhale, hold your breath while imagining the light increasing and radiating throughout your entire being, then exhale while imagining the light radiating from you. If you breathe deeply, breathe normally after each exhale to avoid hyperventilating.

3. When you feel ready, follow Steps 4 and 5 of the instructions for meditation according to your choice for the specific stage of the trip.
4. Repeat Step 2 above and conclude with Steps 6, 7, and 8 of the instructions for meditation.

Meditate with knowledge that the process will yield results but without attachment to any particular result. When illumination comes, it usually comes after meditation while we are in the midst of life. It may come as a heightened awareness of our habitual approach or reaction to events. It may come as recognition of any egocentric tendencies that are delaying our progress toward Bethlehem. Incidentally, a particularly prevalent but deceptive egocentric tendency that delays us is the belief that achieving peace of mind signals the end of the mystical journey. Remembering that Jerusalem, which symbolizes peace of mind, is the abode of Herod, we know that we must move beyond it to find the Christ child within us.

Sometimes illumination after meditation comes in the form of a dream, a series of dreams, or fantasies that occur spontaneously when we are awake. In dreams or fantasies, archetypes appear as real persons, mythical or other fictitious characters, animals or objects that have meaning for the dreamer or fantasizer. For instance, a particularly respected teacher or friend or a famous scientist or philosopher might represent the magician or wise man archetype; a modern-day dictator or despotic business tycoon might represent the evil king archetype. Information would be conveyed through the archetype's words or actions and his or her effect on us both during the dream or fantasy and afterward.

Particularly significant dreams and fantasies tend to call attention to themselves. They may feature vivid colors or be outrageously absurd; they may be frightening or exceptionally dramatic or extremely frustrating. In some way, they will make a strong impression that will linger for a while after waking consciousness returns.

Because dreams and fantasies or visions have always been a way in which God has guided spiritual searchers, it is a good practice for persons who are serious about the mystical trip to keep a journal of dreams and fantasies and to spend time thinking about each one. The material in the previous chapters should help interpret those dreams and fantasies that follow meditative work on stages of the trip to Bethlehem. A spiritual counselor can often help too. However, the best interpretation is always the one that feels right to the dreamer and has a transformative effect upon the individual's consciousness.

10

Stage Three
Understanding: Embodying Grace

Although Stages One and Two are preparation for the trip, they also continue throughout the journey. In Stage One we deny power to the egocentric ego and in Stage Two we become open to the "wisdom from above" (James 3:17). Both are necessary throughout our lives. Indeed, every stage is a continuing process, for the trip to Bethlehem is never entirely completed.

During each of the next four stages, specific aspects of the thinking and feeling natures begin their journey toward Bethlehem, the point in consciousness where the Christ or higher Self emerges.

Stage Three starts the actual transformation of consciousness by revealing our potential for embodying grace. Grace is the generous love and mercy of God that are always active. We experience God's grace whenever we do not suffer the consequences of our own negative thoughts, words, or deeds or when what we have feared does not happen. We experience God's grace whenever we receive an unexpected and, so far as we can see, undeserved blessing.

Gabriel's appearance at the right side of the altar to tell Zechariah that despite his and Elizabeth's age, they will produce a son is an instance of grace as an unexpected blessing. That the child is to be named John (which means "grace") signifies that it is God's gracious will that we also express grace in our dealings with one another and with all parts of our inner selves. When love as the awareness of our essential oneness with other people and mercy govern our dealings with them, we acquire the illumined intellect that forms conscience or the moral nature. Metaphysically, John the Baptist represents both the illumined intellect and the moral nature.

Formerly, it was thought that God's grace could be expressed only through noble persons or those especially favored by God. The fact that John is the child of two elderly human parents symbolizes that humanity has now matured enough to develop a new moral nature so that anyone can be a channel for grace.

Because through the Christ we have access to infinite power, it is essential that the illumined intellect and new moral nature emerge first. If we could avail ourselves of the Christ power without them, the egocentric ego would become inflated and, in all probability, lead us to misuse that power solely for our own benefit. As the forerunner of the Christ, the inner John the Baptist protects one from ego inflation; both the error of considering oneself the one and only expression of the Christ and the consequences of misusing the power of the Christ.

Just as important, perhaps even more important, is the need for us to understand that we must deal lovingly and mercifully with every aspect of our psyche. Even those parts of us that we have formerly suppressed or rejected, those parts that make up what Carl Jung calls the "shadow," must be accepted and integrated into consciousness so that we can direct their vital energy toward individuation, the psychological process by which Jung says we move toward wholeness, toward our unique expression of the higher Self. Considered from the spiritual standpoint, individuation leads to individualized expression of the Christ.

The aged Elizabeth's conception of John symbolizes that it is never too late for our feeling nature to nurture the idea of grace until it is incorporated into our moral nature. As we gain greater understanding of ourselves and treat all aspects of our own being with love and mercy, we are better able to extend grace to others. Gradually we realize, as Jesus taught, that despite outer differences, we all have the same infinite potential. That realization is further protection from ego inflation. The illumined intellect prepares us to see that what we like or dislike in ourselves, we like or dislike in others. We can then understand that we are to judge behavior and not persons.

For this stage of the mystical trip, select the method you will use for meditation. It need not be the same one used at Stage Two; however, it is wise to use the brief meditation upon the star at the beginning.

Because gold is the color associated with understanding, using golden light for the meditation is suggested.

Quotations for Grace

"... Grace is poured upon your lips; therefore God has blessed you for ever."—Psalm 45:2

"... Surely goodness and mercy shall follow me all the days of my life ..."—Psalm 23:6

"He that followeth after righteousness and mercy findeth life, righteousness, and honour."—Proverbs 21:21 KJV

"... What does the Lord require of you but to do justice, and to love kindness, and to walk humbly with your God?"—Micah 6:8

"Render true judgments, show kindness and mercy ..." —Zechariah 7:9

"Blessed are the merciful, for they shall obtain mercy." —Matthew 5:7

Quotations for Understanding

"... It is the spirit in a man, the breath of the Almighty, that makes him understand."—Job 32:8

"[Gabriel] said to me, ' ... I have now come out to give you wisdom and understanding ... for you are greatly beloved; therefore consider the word and understand the vision.'"—Daniel 9:22-23

"... Understand what the will of the Lord is ..."—Ephesians 5:17

"... The Lord will grant you understanding in everything ..." —2 Timothy 2:7

Affirmations for Grace and Understanding

As I nurture the grace of God within me, I move toward Bethlehem.
The Spirit of God illumines my understanding.
I judge and treat all aspects of my being with love and mercy.
I judge and treat others with love and mercy.
As I radiate love and mercy, love and mercy return to bless me.

Meditation for Grace and Understanding

In the sanctuary, my inner priest burns incense at the altar. The fragrant smoke rises like my prayer for illumination, for I would know the Truth. I wait in silence for a time. Then a voice speaks in the sanctuary, astounding the inner priest: "It is never too late to let thought and feeling combine to bring forth a new moral nature. You can express divine grace. Let knowledge of the law be illumined by the light of God's love. Deal mercifully with yourself and with all persons, even as God deals mercifully with you."

Meditate in silence upon God's gifts of grace and understanding.

11

Stage Four
Imagination: Glimpsing the Christ

During Stage Four, the implications of our Christ potential glimpsed in Stage Two are revealed to the feeling nature. During Stage Two, we see the Christ potential as a spiritual goal for our religious life, but during Stage Four, we begin to imagine its transformative effect upon all aspects of the self or soul—the total consciousness. Though we may think ourselves unready because we have not yet figured out intellectually how to find and express the higher Self (Mary's saying, "How can this be, since I have no husband?") or how it fits into our existing religious convictions, we realize that God's activity in the soul undergoing purification is more powerful than the human intellect. God can do for us what we cannot do for ourselves. Moreover, because the intellect is already being illumined and the new moral nature is coming into being, the idea of grace is established in consciousness (the sixth month of Elizabeth's pregnancy). The conditions have been met to make it possible and safe for the imagination to give form to the idea of a transformed consciousness.

The faculty of imagination plays a crucial part in any creative endeavor, for it is the ability to actually conceive the possibility of any new thing or condition. As we hold to the idea of the new, it gathers more and more mental or spiritual energy, until it impels us to bring it into manifestation. Nothing is more creative than our transformation from being merely human into being human expressions of the Christ. When the imagination conceives and focuses on the Christ idea, the whole activity of God (the Holy Spirit) works to bring it into manifestation.

Because imagination has no apparent limits, the color associated with it is sky blue or light blue. Amethyst is the color associated with the idea of advanced spiritual growth. Either color may be used at this stage.

Quotations for Imagination

"... God speaks ... in a dream, in a vision of the night ..."—Job 33:14-15

"... I shall see the goodness of the Lord in the land of the living!"—Psalm 27:13

"... Whatever is true, whatever is honorable, whatever is just, whatever is pure, whatever is lovely, whatever is gracious, if there is any excellence, if there is anything worthy of praise, think about these things."—Philippians 4:8

Affirmations for Imagination

I conceive the idea of my inner Christ; I believe in my inner Christ; I can achieve expression of my inner Christ.
My imagination is my creative power.
I hold the vision of myself as a beloved (son, daughter) of God.
I imagine only the highest and best in me and all people.
Through imagination, I am God's coworker in my transformation.

Meditation for Imagination

Focus upon the center of your being and imagine this scene within you.
In a quiet room just before dawn, a maiden stirs from sleep, wakened by the sense of a presence. Her eyelids flutter open and she pushes herself onto her elbows. An iridescent glow fills her sight. As she watches in wonder, a shimmering form of an angel appears and greets her saying,

"Hail, O favored one, the Lord is with you!" Puzzled and a little fearful, she stares at the vision. It speaks again: "Do not be afraid, Mary, for you have found favor with God." Listening in amazement, she learns that she is to bear the Son of God, the Messiah who "will reign over the house of Jacob for ever." Mary, not yet married but only betrothed to Joseph, protests, "How shall this be, since I have no husband?" The angel replies that the activity of God within her is responsible for the holy Being. Then the angel tells her that her elderly cousin, though formerly barren, is now six months pregnant and adds, "For with God nothing will be impossible." Assured that God is with her, Mary says, "Behold, I am the handmaid of the Lord; let it be to me according to your word."

As the vision fades, know that Mary is your soul and the words are meant for you. If you are willing, the seed of God's own image in your soul will unfold to govern every aspect of your being and transform you.

$$\boxed{12}$$

Stage Five
Faith: Trusting the Good

In Stage Five of the mystical trip, faith becomes strong. Faith is our ability to believe and trust that God's will is for our highest good even before the good has appeared in our lives. Mary's hasty departure to visit Elizabeth for three months at her home in the hills of Judah symbolizes the impulse to test the validity of an intuitively received idea, particularly when it seems impossible. The angelic message is validated when Mary sees for herself that Elizabeth is pregnant. Her faith has been justified and strengthened, as indicated by her prayer known as the "Magnificat" in Luke 1:46-55, which begins, "My soul magnifies the Lord, and my spirit rejoices in God my Savior ..." Remember, too, that a hill town in Judah symbolizes a high state of praise and the house of a priest represents traditional religious consciousness. Mary's three-month visit also symbolizes that, within a traditional religious consciousness, one can persist in prayer until the feeling nature has fully integrated the energy of love (represented by Elizabeth) into consciousness and the new moral nature is ready to become active in daily life.

A clear, deep blue is the color associated with faith. In many representations of the Virgin Mary, she wears a deep blue robe.

Quotations for Faith

"According to your faith be it done to you."—Matthew 9:29

"... If you have faith as a grain of mustard seed ... nothing will be impossible to you."—Matthew 17:20

"All things are possible to him who believes ..."—Mark 9:23

"... Whatever you ask in prayer, believe that you receive it, and you will."—Mark 11:24 RSVCE

Affirmations for Faith

The grace of God within me strengthens my faith.
My faith in God sustains me on my journey to Bethlehem.
By faith, I am healed, prospered, and transformed.
My soul is filled with faith.
Faith works miracles within me.
With faith in God, I express my Christ nature.

Meditations for Faith

Two different meditations are suggested for Stage Five. In the first one, featuring Mary and Elizabeth, faith strengthens as the feeling nature and is infused with a sense of God's transformative power. In the second, featuring Zechariah, the neighbors, and kinsfolk, faith strengthens further as the thinking nature and completely accepts the idea that God will help people express their capacity for love and mercy in their daily lives.

Meditation One: Mary climbs a steep pathway up a bleached hillside against a deep blue sky to a stone house, the home of Zechariah and Elizabeth. Though she is weary, her face glows with the excitement of mixed emotions as she nears the door. If the angel spoke the truth about Elizabeth, Mary will share the angel's message for the first time. Will Elizabeth believe? What will Zechariah say?

She stands at the door and calls out a greeting. The door opens and before she can say another word, Elizabeth, obviously with child, is there, saying, "Blessed are you among women, and blessed is the fruit of your womb!" Elizabeth already knows, and the angel told the truth. Glad thanksgiving banishes doubt, and Mary bursts into a joyous prayer: "My soul magnifies the Lord, and my spirit rejoices in God my Savior ... for he has done great things for me ..."

Meditate upon faith in God's power to do great things for you.

Meditation Two: Here I stand, surrounded by neighbors and kinsfolk who come to rejoice with Elizabeth and me over the birth of our son and to witness the rites that mark him as one of God's children. I cannot speak, for I was silenced until God's will was done.

There is still one thing to do, to name the child. The people would call him after me, a priest, but Elizabeth says, "Not so; he shall be called John." It is the name the angel gave, which I wrote for Elizabeth. They turn to me, and on a tablet I write again, "His name is John."

And lo! My speech returns as I praise God: "Blessed be the Lord God of Israel, for he has visited and redeemed his people ... And you, child, will be called the prophet of the Most High; for you will go before the Lord to prepare his ways, to give knowledge of salvation to his people in the forgiveness of their sins, through the tender mercy of our God ..."

In silence, accept God's help in expressing grace and faith.

13

Stage Six
Will: Making the Choice

During Stage Six, we overcome much of our reluctance to change as we choose to allow God's will to be done in and through us. Will is the faculty through which we make choices. Our choices determine the direction our lives will take. To choose to discover and do God's will for us is the proper use of will in every area of our lives. That choice is most important to the process of transformation for then we are ready to do whatever is required to allow the higher Self to emerge and take its rightful place as the governing center of consciousness. This is a stage to which we return every time any vestige of the egocentric ego begins to reassert itself.

To remind us of the value of will, the color assigned to this faculty is silver gray.

Quotations for Will

"You will decide on a matter, and it will be established for you, and light will shine on your ways."—Job 22:28

"Thy will be done, on earth as it is in heaven ..."—Matthew 6:10

"... Father ... not as I will, but as thou wilt."—Matthew 26:39

"... It is your Father's good pleasure to give you the kingdom."—Luke 12:32

"My food is to do the will of him who sent me, and to accomplish his work."—John 4:34

Affirmations for Will

Willingly, I accept God's will for my highest good.
It is God's will that I express my spiritual nature.
I will to do the will and work of God in me and in my world.
I let God's will for good be done in and through me.

Meditation for Will

Christ waiting to be born in me! How could that be? Like Joseph when Mary said she was pregnant with God's child, I first wanted to be rid of the idea, but now I am ready to let God speak to me. I am like the young Samuel, who said, "Speak, Lord, for thy servant hears." I choose to open my mind to the wisdom of God and to let God's will for me guide my will.

In silence, surrender to God's will.

14

Stage Seven
Strength:
Persisting with Purpose

Until Stage Seven, the Christ idea is a growing possibility that has captured the imagination and the attention of the thinking and feeling natures; at the end of this stage, although it emerges as the central factor of consciousness, it is still as in need of nurture and protection as a newborn babe. Fortunately, by the time it emerges, the faculty of strength has become spiritually active. Mary and Joseph's required trek from Nazareth to Bethlehem to enroll for the census represents persistence in prayer and meditation, which keeps thoughts and feelings focused on our spiritual purpose even while we fulfill our pressing worldly obligations (symbolized by the census).

Many of the other people who would also have made such a trip and crowded the inn represent other thoughts and feelings connected to the city of David (consciousness of faith and love active in human life). They increase the flow of strength. However, as in any inn, some people would be foreigners who were not there for the census; they represent thoughts and feelings not related to faith and love or the spiritual purpose. The inn, therefore, represents a mixed and confused consciousness in which the spiritual birth cannot occur. Going into the stable-cave (symbol of the unconscious) represents going within ourselves in meditation to achieve the harmonious state in which awareness of the spiritual identity can emerge.

Though destined to be the central factor of the consciousness, when the idea of the inner Christ first appears, it is like an infant, needing conscious commitment to nurture it (lay it in the manger) and to restrain it (wrap it in swaddling cloths) so that the strength of its infinite potentialities is focused within the individual psyche. Commitment requires persistence, patience, endurance, firm purpose, and stability—all aspects of the faculty of strength that are enhanced when the Christ comes alive in consciousness. The color associated with strength is spring green. It reminds us of the potential strength in early shoots of grass or new leaves.

Quotations for Strength

"The Lord is my strength and my song ..."—Exodus 15:2

"... The joy of the Lord is your strength."—Nehemiah 8:10

"... The God of Israel, he gives power and strength to his people."—Psalm 68:35

"... In quietness and in trust shall be your strength."—Isaiah 30:15

"... They who wait for the Lord shall renew their strength ..." —Isaiah 40:31

"I can do all things in him who strengthens me."— Philippians 4:13

Affirmations for Strength

Strength is my birthright as God's beloved (son, daughter).
As I think of God's love, I feel strong and secure.
God gives me the strength to persevere.
My indwelling Christ fills me with strength.
I am a strong child of God.

Meditation for Strength

Many people trudge along the rocky road that winds through a valley and up to the little city of Bethlehem. In the midst of the weary band, Mary rides an ass led by Joseph. It is dusk when Mary and Joseph arrive at the noisy, crowded inn. At the door, the innkeeper says there is no room, but, seeing Mary's condition, he directs them to the stable, a roomy cave in the hillside where he shelters his docile ox. There is clean, sweet-smelling hay for the ass and enough to make beds for the tired travelers. Far from the noisy inn, they can rest quietly.

At midnight, Mary knows her time has come. Gently, she awakens Joseph. He goes out and returns with the innkeeper's wife, who brings a pitcher of water and some salt. She has borne children and helped other mothers and knows what to do. Mary is young and strong, and this is an easy, silent birth. After the custom of the Jews, the innkeeper's wife cuts the cord, then carefully washes and rubs the baby's body with salt and places him in Mary's arms.

Tenderly, Mary ministers to her babe, wrapping him in swaddling cloths, then laying him in the manger beside her before she closes her eyes to rest and renew her strength while Joseph silently keeps watch.

Strength flows into me as I, too, rest in silence.

15

Stage Eight
Love: Realizing Oneness

Stage Eight illustrates the attracting, harmonizing force of divine love—the very nature of God symbolized by the image of God that is represented by the Christ child. Divine love is also the principle of oneness because God is the only presence and power. Awareness of divine love illuminates the greater purpose of the human virtues that express various aspects of human love and are symbolized by sheep. The greater purpose is to help us realize oneness or harmony within ourselves so we can express it in the world.

The shepherds who are watching their flock by night represent forces in the unconscious that guard the seven natural virtues—honesty, prudence, temperance, courage, justice, charity, and compassion—the potential in human beings for expressing oneness with one another.

The angel says that the birth of the child is for them and will bring joy "to all the people," indicating that, with the emergence of the Christ, a profound change occurs in how and toward whom the virtues are to be expressed. Until now, the shepherds have guarded the flock carefully; it is "their flock." The angel's message, together with the chorus of the heavenly host, causes them to leave the flock alone. With the coming of the Christ, we need not fear that we will ever lose the virtues. They can be safely left in God's care, for they belong to God.

Until we have a Stage Eight experience of some kind, we tend to express the virtues mostly in our immediate environment. After we have had a Stage Eight experience, we are ready to express the virtues toward the whole world. The "glory of the Lord" has shone around us, so to speak, and revealed the presence of the higher Self in the midst of us, regardless of what we call it. Having found it within ourselves, we can recognize its presence in others and discover our essential oneness with all humanity. This activates divine love, the source of the virtues within us. Divine love creates harmony among parts of ourselves, reconciling the opposites (the ox and ass), so that we can spontaneously and easily express the virtues toward family, friends, foreigners, and even foes.

The gift of the lamb (added by tradition to Luke's account of the nativity) symbolizes the harmlessness of the Christ. The Christ is pure, innocent, sweet, and forgiving. It will do no harm or violence within us nor lead us to harm anyone else. To the contrary, its birth in us increases the ability to channel grace and makes us God's partners in the manifestation of peace on earth.

The color associated with love is pink, as we observe on Valentine's Day.

Quotations for Love

"O give thanks to the Lord, for he is good; for his steadfast love endures for ever!"—1 Chronicles 16:34

"Steadfast love and faithfulness will meet; righteousness and peace will kiss each other."—Psalm 85:10

"Love your enemies and pray for those who persecute you ..."—Matthew 5:44

"You shall love the Lord your God with all your heart, and with all your soul, and with all your strength, and with all your mind; and your neighbor as yourself."—Luke 10:27

"... Nor height, nor depth, nor anything else in all creation, will be able to separate us from the love of God in Christ Jesus our Lord."—Romans 8:39

"Beloved, let us love one another; for love is of God, and he who loves is born of God and knows God ... for God is love."—1 John 4:7-8

Affirmations for Love

I am God's beloved, lovable, loving child.

Through the Christ in me, I am a radiating center of divine love.

As an expression of divine love, I send forth love and attract love.

God is love; I am one with God; I am one with love.

Through the love of God, I am transformed.

Meditation for Love

For this meditation, imagine that you are the youngest shepherd, a lad of 13.

It is a starry midnight on a hill near Bethlehem. I am old enough to be out in the fields with my father and kinsmen to guard the flock from animals and thieves. I stood early watch. How proud I was to guard the sheep, for they are the wealth of my family. Now it is my turn to sleep.

I curl in my cloak near the fire, just drifting into sleep. Suddenly a bright light forces my eye open. Before us is a brilliant figure, an angel. We grasp one another, huddling together. In a voice as sweet as music, the angel says, "Be not afraid. I bring you good news of a great joy which will come to all the people; for to you is born this day in the city of David a Savior, who is Christ the Lord." He says we will find the baby wrapped in swaddling cloths and lying in a manger. Then a heavenly choir chants, "Glory to God in the highest, and on earth peace among men ..." The light fades and the angel disappears.

I pinch myself. I am not dreaming. I get up as the others scramble to their feet saying, "Let us go over to Bethlehem and see this thing that has happened, which the Lord has made known to us." I think someone should stay with the sheep, but my father says they will be safe because God wants us to see the baby. He puts a lamb in my arms, a gift for the child.

We hurry to the city. A light in the stable-cave near the inn seems to beckon us. A man appears at the mouth of the cave. We tell him about the angel, and he invites us in. We enter quietly. Beside the manger, a young woman sits. She signals us to come nearer. I lay the lamb at her feet near the manger and look in to see the sleeping child, and my heart fills with love.

As we return to the flock, we sing a psalm of joy.

In silence, let love and joy fill you.

16

Stage Nine
Order: Keeping a Balance

Scenes from Stages Seven, Eight, and Ten are the most familiar and appealing parts of the traditional Christmas story. Stage Seven features the journey to Bethlehem, the crowded inn, and the birth of the child. Stage Eight features the visit of the shepherds and Stage Ten the visit of the wise men. Yet although it is less familiar, when understood from the metaphysical point of view, Stage Nine is an important part of the transformation process. The dedication of the child in the temple at Jerusalem in the presence of Simeon and Anna is as significant as the birth itself, for the events symbolize commitment to the nurture and expression of the Christ.

Stage Nine illustrates the proper sequence for inner events following the emergence of the Christ. This important function of the faculty of order gives service to God first priority in our lives.

On the eighth day (symbolizing the beginning of a new life cycle of rebirth and regeneration that will endure), Mary and Joseph circumcise and name the baby. As with the circumcision of John, the rite signifies both renunciation of lower desires (such as greed, lust, selfish ambition, and the urge to control other people) and total acceptance of the Christ as a part of the religious consciousness. Giving the child the God-ordained name Jesus or *Joshua* symbolizes the thinking nature's recognition of the Christ as the spiritual factor that saves us from error, heals us on all levels, and prospers us in the highest meaning of the word.

There follows a two-month period during which, according to the traditional story, Joseph moved the family into a house (symbolizing the thinking nature's full acceptance of the Christ) to take proper care of Mary and the baby. Just as the welfare of any mother and newborn infant should have priority in a household, the welfare of the soul and the emergent Christ should have priority and claim the center of consciousness. *Two* months symbolizes an indeterminate time needed for the achievement of inner equilibrium. This equilibrium is reached by balancing conventional religious thoughts with spiritual feelings and aspirations and occurs when the higher Self is the center of consciousness.

At the end of that time, Mary and Joseph go to Jerusalem to fulfill religious law by dedicating Jesus to the Lord in the temple. In this instance, the temple in Jerusalem indicates that both mind and body are at peace when the higher Self is dedicated to the service of God. The sacrifice offered symbolizes the placement of our capacity for fidelity, gentleness, peace, and high aspiration at the service of God. The presence and blessings of Simeon and Anna indicate that the thinking and feeling natures have been imbued with spiritual wisdom.

The events of this stage culminate in our firm commitment to the service of God through expression of the Christ.

A deep, clear green is the color associated with order, probably because it is the color of most mature leaves, which result from orderly growth.

Quotations for Order

"For everything there is a season, and a time for every matter under heaven ..."—Ecclesiastes 3:1

"... First the blade, then the ear, then the full grain in the ear."—Mark 4:28

"... All things should be done decently and in order."—1 Corinthians 14:40

Affirmations for Order

Divine order governs my transformation from what I seem to be into what I truly am: an expression of God's image.
As I express my spiritual nature, divine order governs my life.
I do all things in divine order.
I commit myself to God's service through my Christ nature.

Meditation for Order

Identify with Joseph for this meditation.

The coming of this child changes everything. From now on, what he and his mother need command my attention. It is a sweet service, for they are gentle and undemanding.

We have performed the ancient rite to acknowledge God's everlasting promise to watch over us. We have given the child the name God chose, Jesus. The name is right, for peace and assurance radiate from this child.

Now we are in the temple. An old man with a joyful face draws near and takes the child in his arms. He blesses God and says that the child is "a light for revelation to the Gentiles, and for glory to ... Israel." Then he warns Mary that the child will be "spoken against" and that she will know sorrow. Of course, that is true. Everyone can be unjustly treated and every mother knows sorrow at such times. Then an ancient woman, a prophetess devoted to God, comes forward too. She praises God for sending the child and foretells great good. Only the wisdom of God could reveal such things to them.

As they leave, I do what the law requires. I declare the child holy to the Lord and make the thank-offering in pledge of faithfulness to God's trust.

I am at peace, for I know that when I take Mary and Jesus home to Nazareth, God will help me to fulfill my commitment.

In silence, make your commitment to your higher Self.

17

Stage Ten
Power: Finding the King

In Stage Ten, we acquire the poise, self-mastery, and dominion or power over ourselves and circumstances that can come only after we have committed ourselves to expressing the higher Self. Once we have made that commitment, even the egocentric ego (Herod) assists the process, albeit unintentionally. When the accumulated wisdom of the ages or spiritual wisdom (symbolized by the three Magi) arises in a consciousness committed to nurturing the higher Self and serving God, the faculty of power gains a spiritual dimension; it becomes spiritual power.

The gifts of the Magi represent attributes of spiritual power. Gold indicates the enduring value of all spiritual gifts. Frankincense symbolizes the potential for transmutation which, through the wise use of spiritual power, purifies and sanctifies ordinary material life. Myrrh symbolizes not only the underlying serenity or bliss and peace one feels even in the midst of difficulties when spiritual power is active, but also the capacity for love and charisma possessed by such a person.

Purple is the color associated with power, because in early times, purple dye was so costly that only the rich and powerful could afford clothing dyed purple.

Quotations for Power

"God ... gives power and strength to his people."—Psalm 68:35

"Death and life are in the power of the tongue ..."—Proverbs
   18:21

"... I am filled with power, with the Spirit of the Lord ..."—
   Micah 3:8

"... The power of the Most High will overshadow you ..."—
   Luke 1:35

"... You shall receive power when the Holy Spirit has come
   upon you."—Acts 1:8

"For there is no power but of God ..."—Romans 13:1 KJV

Affirmations for Power

God is the only power.
Through the spirit of God in me, I have power.
I use my words carefully, for they are powerful.
As I express the Christ, my power for good increases.

Meditation for Power

Identify with one of the Magi for this meditation.

The long trip is almost over. We found the newborn king, though not
in the royal palace in Jerusalem where we expected to find Him, but in
a humble house in Bethlehem. Hearing of our inquiries, Herod learned
from his scholars that a prophet foretold the birth of the promised king
in Bethlehem. He summoned us. First, he questioned us closely about
the time when we first saw the star, and then he sent us to Bethlehem,
telling us to return to tell him where he could find the child so that he
could pay him homage too. But we felt uneasy.

The star led us to the little city and the house. The father invited us to
enter.

I can relive that visit to the little room at will. The lovely young mother
holds out the glowing child in her arms. In love and awe, we kneel, for
we are in the presence of the holy Being that belongs to us and all people.
We open the gifts—gold, frankincense, and myrrh, those signs of royal
power—and lay them at her feet. The child smiles, and we are blessed.

That night, each of us awoke from a warning dream. We were not to return to Herod. He must not find the child. Before dawn, we mounted our camels and rode away, not through Jerusalem, but by the other route. The child would be safe.

Now we are almost home. Our hearts are filled with joy. Faithfully we have followed the star, and we have found the king.

In silence, accept the inflow of spiritual power.

18

Stage Eleven
Zeal: Catching Fire

In Stages Eleven and Twelve, we perform the responsibilities to the higher Self and allow all our spiritual faculties to help us to fulfill them.

During Stage Eleven, we realize that, though the egocentric ego poses the major threat to the higher Self, the faculty of zeal equips us to protect it. In Stage Twelve, the faculty of life helps us make the higher Self the vitalizing force in our ordinary, everyday experience.

Like all the spiritual faculties, zeal has been active to some degree for as long as we have been alive and certainly from the beginning of the mystical trip to Bethlehem. However, during Stage Eleven, zeal takes the lead.

As an attribute of God, zeal is the eternal activity that creates and sustains everything that appears and impels each thing toward fulfillment of the divine idea from which it originates. Zeal has been called God's "unbroken flow of life" and "unremitting activity."[1]

When active on the strictly material level, the faculty of zeal gives us the ability to concentrate attention and effort upon a project until we have seen it through to completion. But zeal can also be no more than hectic enthusiasm that fizzles out rapidly. Its effect can be either constructive or destructive. When not balanced with love, wisdom, and understanding, sustained zeal becomes fanaticism. As a spiritual faculty, zeal acts in concert with other faculties and enables us to respond fully to inspiration from God by directing mental, emotional, and physical resources toward the realization of God's purposes. Then zeal is "the inward fire" or divine enthusiasm that motivates us to do whatever we must do to cooperate with the creative activity of God and to express our own higher Self.

The principal action of every character, including Herod, in the Christmas story illustrates some aspect of zeal. In Stage Eleven, Herod demonstrates the use of zeal as a strictly material faculty. His massacre of the infants illustrates the terrible consequences wrought by zeal when one directs it toward a selfish purpose. His use of zeal exemplifies the lengths to which the egocentric ego will go to protect its own position. It will try to eliminate any idea that bears any resemblance to the Christ. Joseph's action, however, demonstrates the use of zeal as a spiritual faculty.

Joseph receives inspiration in a dream and, without hesitation, he responds. He willingly does what he is guided to do to protect and nurture the child and contribute to its growth and development. That, of course, exemplifies what happens when the spiritually inspired intellect uses zeal. When the faculties are spiritually balanced and zeal is active, we do not need to depend upon only our limited human intellect, for God will guide us every step of the way. Orange, a mixture of yellow and red, is the color associated with zeal, indicating that as a spiritual faculty it blends wisdom and life in equal amounts.

Quotations for Zeal

"For to us a child is born ... and the government will be upon his shoulder ... from this time forth and for evermore. The zeal of the Lord of hosts will do this."—Isaiah 9:6-7

"I have filled him with the Spirit of God ..."—Exodus 31:3

"... He will baptize you with the Holy Spirit and with fire."—Matthew 3:11

"... He will be filled with the Holy Spirit ..."—Luke 1:15

"... Know the love of Christ ... be filled with all the fulness of God."—Ephesians 3:19

Affirmations for Zeal

The zeal of God inspires me to divine right action.
Zeal is my inward fire; wisdom directs it for spiritual growth.
With zeal, love, and wisdom, I do what needs to be done by me.
I am filled with the spirit of God.

Meditation for Zeal

Identify with Joseph for this meditation.

As the three men from the East rode into the night on their camels, I stood at the door and watched. I was awed by the tale they had told of following the star and by the gifts they had given. Indeed, God had entrusted someone precious to my care. So far, all was well. Surely God was watching over us. I felt secure as I lay down. Mary and Jesus were peacefully asleep before I closed my eyes.

Then I had a dream. Gabriel appeared and told me to arise and take them to Egypt because Herod would be searching for the child to destroy Him. I awoke and roused Mary, for I knew the message had come from God. At the least hint of a rival, Herod would act. He had done so with his own family. We must waste no time.

Mary did not protest. Quietly, she gathered only the necessities for herself and the child and bundled their clothes while I gathered mine and readied the ass. Then we set off under the midnight sky and were far from Bethlehem when the sun rose.

It was a long trip but surprisingly easy. We rested by day and set off at sunset until we crossed the border. Though I was taking my family into a strange land, I was not afraid. Had not God given us the stars to guide us? I needed only to look up to see the way we were to go each night. And so we arrived safely in a village where people were happy to have a new carpenter and his family settle among them.

As it is written in scripture, "In all your ways acknowledge him, and he will make straight your paths" (Proverbs 3:6).

Meditate on the verse from Proverbs.

19

Stage Twelve
Life: Nurturing the Christ

At the end of Stage Twelve, though not yet mature, the Christ is alive and growing. Hidden in the depths of the psyche (Egypt), it is protected by the thinking nature and nurtured by the feeling nature until the old egocentric ego loses all power to harm it. At the same time, the growing inner Christ stimulates all spiritual faculties to greater activity, for the preservation of the Christ idea is the work of the faculty of life. In the mind of God, life is the unceasing creative activity within all things, which impels them toward realization of the divine idea they are designed to express. As a spiritual power in us, the faculty of life directs the work of all the other faculties toward the full development of the higher Self, the Christ idea we are designed to express.

Of course, life has been at work through all the symbolic stages of the mystical trip, but in Stage Twelve the protection and nurture of the higher or Christ Self has priority.

The color associated with life is red, the color of blood.

Quotations for Life

"The spirit of God has made me, and the breath of the
   Almighty gives me life."—Job 33:4

"Thou dost show me the path of life ..."—Psalm 16:11

"The fruit of the righteous is a tree of life ..."—Proverbs 11:30

"The teaching of the wise is a fountain of life ..."—Proverbs
   13:14

"... As the Father has life in himself, so he has granted the Son also to have life in himself."—John 5:26

"... The free gift of God is eternal life ..."—Romans 6:23

Affirmations for Life

God is eternal life.

Daily, I walk in the newness of life.

I am an expression of God's eternal life.

Through me, God lives, moves, and expresses being.

Meditation for Life

Imagine the Christ within you speaking to you.

I came that you may have life and have it abundantly. You have welcomed me into your mind and heart and made me the center of your being. You and I are one, for I love you with an everlasting love. From now on, the gifts from the Magi are yours. You attract to you all that you need to live as the child of God that you are, for as I am one with God and you are one with me, you are one with God. Wherever you are, God is with you as God is with Me. You can face each day with confidence and courage, for the power to meet and grow through every challenge is now yours. God is the life of your body and soul. That life vivifies all your spiritual gifts. The riches of Spirit pour into you. You may seem to live an ordinary life but hidden deep within you is the wellspring of eternal life. Be at peace.

20

Live the Story

Anyone of any religion may take the mystical trip because, regardless of the name by which one knows it, the higher Self is an archetype, the central potential in the psyche of every human being. Moreover, though specific religions are human constructions, the urge to construct them is in response to the powerful archetype of Spirit—the Ultimate Power that creates, governs, and is intimately involved with all that is. Religious practices are designed to bring about a conscious relationship between the higher Self and the Ultimate Power.

To us, that Ultimate Power is known as God. Though Spirit or God is infinite and eternal, God is ever-present within creation as the source of all life or energy and activity. God is the matrix of creation and the substance of every created thing.

God is also the One Mind or intelligence of which all other minds are focal points. The intelligence of God is within all things and governs the activity within every material thing so that even photons and subatomic particles "know" how to form and maintain the elements that make up everything from molecules and cells to animal and human bodies and stars.

Whatever exists is an expression of a divine idea in the One Mind. The true purpose, then, of anything is to express as fully as possible the divine idea of itself. Every divine idea contains God-energy that constantly presses toward manifestation. In traditional Christian theology, that omnipresent God-energy is the third person or aspect of God known as the Holy Spirit. It is always active, so we may be confident God is at work within us to help us fulfill God's purpose for us.

Our relationship with God is already established, for although we are in material bodies, we are spiritual beings, each designed to give individualized expression to the Christ. The urge to express the spiritual image of God is a spiritual urge, not necessarily confined to followers of any particular religion. The urge is the God-energy pressing toward manifestation. We may call the urge the purpose of God.

Created to express the image of God, we are created to be God's coworkers as we participate in the creation of ourselves. In other words, the seventh day of creation has not yet arrived. God has not yet rested. God is still at work, helping us to do our part. When we deliberately undertake the trip to our spiritual Bethlehem, we respond to the purpose of God. So we may set out confidently, knowing that we are called according to God's purpose. God helps and guides us when we commit to live the Christmas story and take our transformative trip to Bethlehem.

Glossary

Affirmation: a positive statement

Archetype: in Jungian psychology, innate but figurative representations of possible and potential forms of human behavior existing in the collective unconscious mind and thus available to all human minds

Christ: the spiritual image of God within any human being

Collective unconscious: the part of the psyche that retains and transmits the common psychological inheritance of humankind

Denial: a statement that an unwanted or negative thing, circumstance, or condition has no power

Divine idea: a pattern for anything in the Mind of God

Ego: the sense of self

Egocentric: self-centered

Fact: any thing or event that can or could be experienced through bodily senses

Hidden immortal: reference to the spiritual component in human beings

Individuation: according to Jung, the psychological process by which human beings move toward their unique expression of the higher Self

Literal meaning: the obvious or factual meaning of what is said or written

Matter: that which occupies space and that we experience through bodily senses

Messiah: the expected deliverer of the Jews; a title given to Jesus by Christians

Metaphysical meaning: the symbolic or spiritual significance of persons, places, things, and events in life or literature

Metaphysics: the search for first principles or spiritual truth

Moral meaning: in a story, the implied or stated lesson about the consequences of human choices and behavior

Myth: a symbolic story pointing to Truth

Photon: a quantum of light

Race consciousness: the totality of the laws governing physical existence that the human race has formed from its experience

Race mind: the totality of beliefs, thoughts, memories, feelings, and experiences of the human race

Religion: a system of beliefs, rules, and practices designed to bring human beings into whatever is considered a right relationship with the deity or deities of a particular group

Shadow: in Jungian psychology, the combined tendencies and attributes (either positive or negative) that an individual has rejected or repressed

Soul: the individualized expression of the Spirit of God in a human being

Spiritual metaphysics: the search for and study of the principles of spiritual Truth

Spiritually oriented: living in harmony with Truth as it is personally understood

Truth: spelled with a capital "T," unchanging divine principles governing everything, visible and invisible

Notes

Chapter 1: This Is Our Story

[1] Carl G. Jung, *Man and His Symbols*, pp. 21, 89.

[2] Joseph L. Henderson in *Man and His Symbols*, p. 107.

[3] Joseph Campbell, *The Power of the Myth*, pp. 22, 59.

[4] Ira Progoff in *Myths, Dreams, and Religion*, p. 176.

[5] Race consciousness, the totality of human laws, is a function of race mind.

[6] Jung, *Four Archetypes*, p. 55.

Chapter 2: The Myth Is Created

[1] Will Durant, *Caesar and Christ*, p. 558.

[2] Dale C. Allison, Jr., "What Was the Star that Guided the Magi?" p. 20.

[3] Campbell, *The Mythic Image*, p. 33.

Chapter 3: The Traditional (Blended) Christmas Story

[1] Direct quotes are from the Revised Standard Version of the Bible.

Chapter 4: The Journey, Time, and Places

[1] John A. Sanford (ed.), *Fritz Kunkel: Selected Writings*, pp. 106-128.

[2] Charles Fillmore, *Metaphysical Bible Dictionary*, p. 274.

[3] Durant, p. 531.

Chapter 5: The Symbols

[1] G. A. Gaskell, *Dictionary of All Scriptures and Myths*, p. 270.

[2] Jann Aldredge Clanton, *In Whose Image?: God and Gender*, p. 22.

[3] Fillmore, *The Revealing Word*, p. 87.

Chapter 6: The Characters

[1] Fillmore, *Metaphysical Bible Dictionary*, p. 677.

Chapter 8: Stage One: Renunciation: Weakening Egocentricity
[1] Sanford, pp. 106-128.

Chapter 18: Stage Eleven: Zeal: Catching Fire
[1] Ella Pomeroy, *Powers of the Soul,* p. 139.

Bibliography

Achtemeier, Paul J. et al. (eds.), *Harper's Bible Dictionary*, Harper & Row, San Francisco, 1985.

Allison, Dale C., Jr., "What Was the Star that Guided the Magi?" *Bible Review,* December 1993, p. 20.

Beck, William F., *The Christ of the Gospels*, Concordia Publishing House, St. Louis, 1959.

Campbell, Joseph, *The Mythic Image*, Princeton Univ. Press, Princeton, 1974.

———, *Myths to Live By*, Bantam Books, New York, 1988.

Campbell, Joseph (ed.), *Myths, Dreams, and Religion*, Dutton, New York, 1970.

———, *The Portable Jung,* Penguin Books, New York, 1971.

Campbell, Joseph, with Bill Moyers, *The Power of the Myth*, Doubleday, New York, 1988.

Cirlot, J. E., *A Dictionary of Symbols*, 2nd ed., Philosophical Library, New York, 1971.

Clanton, Jann Aldredge, *In Whose Image?: God and Gender*, Crossroad, New York, 1990.

Deikman, Arthur J., *The Observing Self: Mysticism and Psychotherapy*, Beacon Press, Boston, 1982.

Durant, Will, *Caesar and Christ*, Simon & Schuster, New York, 1944.

Fillmore, Charles, *Metaphysical Bible Dictionary*, Unity Books, Unity Village, Mo., 1931.

———, *Mysteries of Genesis*, rev. ed., Unity Books, Unity Village, Mo., 1944.

———, *The Revealing Word*, Unity Books, Unity Village, Mo., 1959.

Grant, Michael, *Jesus: An Historian's Review of the Gospels*, Charles Scribner's Sons, New York, 1977.

Gaskell, G. A., *Dictionary of All Scriptures and Myths*, The Julian Press, Inc., New York, 1960.

Hall, Calvin S., and Vernon J. Nordby, *A Primer of Jungian Psychology*, New American Library, New York, 1973.

Hall, Manly P., *The Secret Teachings of All Ages*, 13th ed., Philosophical Research Society, Los Angeles, 1962.

Jung, Carl G., *Four Archetypes*, Princeton Univ. Press, Princeton, 1970.

———, *Psyche and Symbol*, Doubleday Anchor Books, Garden City, N.Y., 1958.

Jung, Carl G. (ed.), *Man and His Symbols*, Doubleday & Company, Inc., Garden City, N.Y., 1964.

Jung, Carl G., and C. Kerenyi, *Essays on a Science of Mythology*, Princeton Univ. Press, Princeton, 1969.

Kee, Howard Clark, et al., *Understanding the New Testament*, 2nd ed., Prentice-Hall, Englewood Cliffs, N.J., 1965.

The Lost Books of the Bible and The Forgotten Books of Eden, New American Library, New York, 1974.

Metford, J.C.J., *Dictionary of Christian Lore and Legend*, Thames and Hudson, London, 1983.

New Larousse Encyclopedia of Mythology, Hamlyn, Twickenham, U.K., 1959.

Pearson, Carol S., *The Hero Within*, Harper & Row, San Francisco, 1986.

Pomeroy, Ella, *Powers of the Soul*, Island Press, New York, 1948.

Sanford, John A. (ed.), *Fritz Kunkel: Selected Writings*, Paulist Press, New York, 1984.

Sechrist, Alice Spiers, *A Dictionary of Bible Imagery*, Swedenborg Foundation, Inc., New York, 1973.

Smith, William, *Smith's Bible Dictionary*, Pyramid Books, New York, 1967.

Stamps, David, "What Was the Star of Bethlehem?" *National Wildlife*, December-January 1988, pp. 18-19.

Turner, Elizabeth Sand, *Your Hope of Glory*, Unity Books, Unity Village, Mo., 1959.

Walker, Barbara G., *The Woman's Encyclopedia of Myths and Secrets*, Harper & Row, San Francisco, 1983.

Young, Arthur M., *The Reflexive Universe: Evolution of Consciousness*, Delacorte Press, New York, 1976.

Printed in the U.S.A.

B0210